Invitational Selling™

The Human Connection Advantage

Dr. Dennis Cummins

Published by Anchor Point Press

ANCHOR POINT
— P R E S S —

United States of America

Disclaimer

This book is intended for educational and informational purposes only. The author and publisher make no representations or warranties with respect to the accuracy or completeness of the contents and specifically disclaim any implied warranties of merchantability or fitness for a particular purpose. The strategies and examples shared are based on the author's experience and judgment and may not be suitable for every individual or organization. Results are not guaranteed.

Trademark Notice

Invitational Selling™, Connect → Convey → Convert™, *Invitational Organization™, Invitational Language Library™, and related frameworks, terms, and methodologies are trademarks of Dr. Dennis Cummins. All rights reserved.*

ISBNs

Paperback ISBN: 979-8-9949304-1-0

Hardcover ISBN: 979-8-9949304-2-7

eBook ISBN: 979-8-9949304-0-3

Dedication

This book is dedicated to…

My children, Christopher and Lauren, whose lives have shaped my heart and my purpose. I have learned more from being your father than any classroom or stage could ever offer.

And to **Dr. Karen Jacobson,** whose love, companionship, and unwavering support continue to help me grow into the man and leader I strive to be.

TABLE OF CONTENTS

Foreword

Every so often in business, someone reframes the way we think about influence. Not by adding more noise, but by cutting through it. Not by manipulating people into saying "yes," but by reminding us why real leaders never needed to. Dr. Dennis Cummins has done exactly that with *Invitational Selling*, a book that brings us back to what business has always been about: people.

As Dennis points out in this book, when AI creates sameness, human connection becomes your competitive advantage.

I've spent my entire career pushing leaders to think bigger, act bolder, and stop hiding behind excuses. I've seen sales tactics come and go. I've watched trends rise and fall. And now, I'm watching something entirely new, a world where the volume of AI-generated information has exploded so fast that everything sounds the same: polished, perfect, predictable... and if I'm being honest, forgettable.

We have more tools than ever, but fewer people actually listening, and attention spans are getting shorter. That's why this book matters right now more than ever. Because Dennis isn't just giving us another sales strategy. He's giving us a way to stand out in a marketplace drowning in automated words but starving for genuine connection.

Look, I'm a business guy. I love tools. I love systems. I love data. I love anything that helps us scale and work smarter, not harder. And AI is one hell of a tool. It's changing the way we build, market, and deliver value.

But here's the truth too many people are missing: AI cannot make people trust you.

It can write a pitch, but not the connection behind it. It can analyze a lead but not read the emotion on their face. It can build a sequence but not build rapport. And trust, emotion, and rapport, they're the currency of influence. If people can't or won't trust you, you have no followers. And if you have no followers, you have no one to evangelize your brand.

This book is not anti-AI, it's pro-human. It recognizes that when everyone is using the same technology, the real differentiation isn't the tool but the person using it. *Invitational Selling™* gives leaders, teams, and organizations a competitive advantage AI can't replicate: clarity, emotional safety, partnership, and choice.

People crave autonomy. When you try to persuade them, they push back. When you invite them, they lean in. And in today's world, the fastest way to stand out is to sound, and be, human.

Throughout the book, Dennis breaks down something I've seen in boardrooms my entire career: traditional sales relies on pressure. Pressure works... until it doesn't. And in the AI era, it fails faster than ever.

Why? Because people are burnt out. They're numb to pitches. They can spot manipulation from a mile away. Their brains pick up pressure as a threat, and when the brain senses danger, decision-making shuts down.

But when people feel safe, understood, and respected, their defenses drop. Their clarity increases. Their commitment skyrockets. *Invitational Selling*™ aligns with how people actually think and behave. It's not performance or persuasion. It's partnership.

This book helps you create conversations where people choose the next step, not because you maneuvered them into it, but because they want to take it. That is power. That is influence. That is leadership.

The brilliance behind this book isn't just in its psychology but in its simplicity. Here's the winning formula — the **Connect → Convey → Convert**™ **framework.**

Just three steps. Human. Natural. Repeatable.

Connection says, "I see you."

Convey says, "Let's understand each other."

Invitation says, "Would you like to take the next step?"

That's it.

But mastering it changes everything. It works in sales, leadership, coaching, customer service, recruiting, and even with your own family.

Why? Because it's not a sales method, it's a communication method for the AI era. Dennis takes decades of work in sales psychology and puts it into a system your entire team can adopt. And he does it without jargon, tricks, or the tired "always be closing" attitude that, while a popular movie line, has no place in modern business.

One of the strongest parts of this book, and one of the reasons I believe every organization should adopt it, is the Invitational Language Library™. This is a practical approach a simple plug-and-play language you can use right now to transform your conversations. Phrases like:

- "If it makes sense, the next step is…"

- "Would you like to explore this further?"

- "I'm not sure if this is right for you, but…"

These are bridges that remove pressure and create choice. When people choose, they commit. And when they commit, they follow through. That's the difference between closing a sale and building a relationship.

What I appreciate most about Dennis's approach is that he doesn't treat AI like a threat. He treats it like an asset if you don't let it replace the very thing that makes you competitive: your humanity.

AI can prepare you, organize your thoughts, and help you scale. But only you can build trust, establish rapport, or invite someone into a meaningful next step.

Your voice is your advantage. Your story is your differentiation. Your sincerity is your strategy. *Invitational Selling*™ gives you the framework to bring all of that forward boldly and confidently.

As you read this book, you'll hear a lot about connection, not because it's soft, but because it's strong. Connection converts. But invitation? Invitation creates commitment. Learning how to invite instead of pressure isn't just good business. It's good leadership and good communication.

The blueprint Dennis Cummins presents is clear, modern, and urgently needed. It's an invitation for business leaders and sales teams to move beyond outdated patterns and step into a new era where technology supports, and human connection transforms, the way we lead, sell, and communicate.

That shift starts with this book.

Jeffrey Hayzlett

Chairman of the C-Suite Network™, Primetime TV & Podcast Host, Keynote Speaker, Best-Selling Author, and Global Business Celebrity

December 10, 2025

INTRODUCTION

Connection Is the New Persuasion.

If there is one thing I have learned after decades of speaking, selling, and helping organizations communicate with more impact, it is this: People do not want to be sold to, but they are absolutely OK with being invited into something that matters.

Here is something many savvy sales professionals, business owners, and corporate leaders already know: the old persuasion-based playbook does not work anymore, especially now that people are overwhelmed, overscheduled, and surrounded by a constant stream of AI-generated messages.

We are living in a time when practically anyone can generate a sales pitch with the help of AI, and ironically, *that is the problem.*

When everything sounds the same, nothing stands out. When nothing feels human, nobody connects.

This book, *Invitational Selling*™, exists because the world needs a more authentic, human, and effective way to communicate, not just to sell, but to lead, influence, and build relationships that create real results.

The foundation for everything you are about to learn began with a simple moment on a beach.

A Glimpse of Where This Started

You will read the full story in Chapter 1 but let me give you a quick preview because it sets the tone for everything that follows.

Years ago, my daughter Lauren, who was blind, asked me to take her around the beach so she could sell some bead bracelets she had made. She held onto my elbow for guidance as we walked through the sand. Because she could not see who was in front of us, she relied on me to describe who we were approaching.

"Dad, who is there?"

I would look ahead and say things like:

"It looks like a dad, his wife, and their daughter."

"A couple in their twenties."

"A group of kids."

And every time I said it, she would reply with complete confidence:
"I got it, Dad."

In that moment, I realized something important.

I was Lauren's artificial intelligence. I was giving her context, information, and insight so she could decide how she wanted to connect with the people we approached.

But what she did next, the way she introduced herself, the confidence in her voice, the clarity of her message, and the genuine warmth she brought into every conversation, none of that was artificial.

That was pure authenticity.

That was pure invitation.

And that moment changed everything I understood about selling, leading, and connecting.

Why This Book Matters Now

AI can write emails, generate proposals, analyze buyer behavior, and even predict what someone might need. That is useful, powerful, and here to stay.

But AI cannot replace:

- Human connection

- Genuine curiosity

- Clarity of purpose

- Confidence in your value

- The warmth of a real invitation

AI can help you understand who you are approaching.

Connection determines how you approach them.

The invitation determines whether they say yes.

This is the core idea behind Invitational Selling™.

Invitational Selling™ is built on one simple principle: the more autonomy you give people in the decision-making process, the more likely they are to take action.

Pressure destroys trust.

Persuasion creates resistance.

Pitching pushes people away.

But an invitation does the opposite.

An invitation creates space.

An invitation opens a door.

An invitation gives people the freedom to choose (people love choosing).

You Are Who This Book Is Written For

If you:

- Lead a sales team

- Carry a quota

- Own a business

- Manage people

- Present ideas

- Influence decisions

- Speak, coach, or teach

- Or simply want to communicate with more confidence and clarity

... then this book is for you.

You do not need to be slick.

You do not need to memorize scripts.

You do not need to pretend to be someone you are not.

You only need to learn how to:

- Build genuine rapport.

- Communicate unique value.

- Invite without pressure.

These three skills will do more for your influence than any closing technique ever could.

Why This Method Works

Invitational Selling™ works because it aligns with how people actually think, feel, and make decisions.

People want to feel:

- Understood.

- Respected.

- Valued.

- In control.

They do not want to be pushed.

They want to *be empowered.*

This method is grounded in neuroscience, behavioral psychology, and years of real-world experience. But at its heart, it is built on something much simpler: selling should feel good for both people, the one inviting and the one deciding.

What You Will Learn

In this book, you will learn how to:

- create a genuine connection from the very first moment.

- communicate your value with clarity and confidence.

- ask questions that build trust instead of pressure.

- tell simple, meaningful stories that land.

- invite people into decisions instead of pushing them toward them.

- reduce resistance by honoring autonomy.

- blend the power of AI with the irreplaceable insight of human connection.

You will also learn how to use Invitational Selling™ across an entire organization, so your culture, your team, and your message all align.

Before We Begin

If you have ever felt uncomfortable with traditional sales tactics ...

If you have ever felt like you had to force a conversation, perform, or persuade ...

If you have ever wished selling and leading could feel more natural and more aligned with who you really are …

Then this book was written for you.

Because selling is not about pressure or persuasion. Selling is simply about inviting someone to take the next step. And when the invitation is clear and authentic, people respond.

I invite you to get started.

CHAPTER 1

A Hot Beach, a Blind Girl,

and a Bag of Bracelets

The Birth of Invitational Selling™

Some lessons arrive in the middle of a boardroom. Others show up at a conference, a seminar, or on a high-stakes sales call. And some lessons come from a place you would never expect.

For me, one of the most powerful lessons I ever learned about selling happened on a hot, crowded beach on the Fourth of July, with my blind daughter holding onto my elbow and a bag full of plastic bead bracelets swinging at her side.

That day didn't just change the way I sold; it changed the way I taught, communicated, and led. It is the moment that became the foundation for everything you will learn in this book.

A Hot Day, Two Entrepreneurs, and One Different Path

It was brutally hot at the beach that Fourth of July. One of those days where the air feels heavy, and the sand is almost too hot to walk on. My kids, Christopher and Lauren, even though they were only nine and ten years old at the time, had always had strong entrepreneurial streaks, and they decided they wanted to try to make some money that day.

Christopher and his friend Tristan headed up to the boardwalk with a collection of painted seashells they had decorated themselves. It wasn't the worst plan in the world, but the boardwalk was a furnace, no shade, no breeze, and not many people looking to buy anything besides cold drinks.

Still, they were determined. They marched up the steps ready to make their fortune.

Lauren, however, had her own idea.

She turned to me, her bag of bead bracelets in hand, and said, "Dad, will you walk me around so I can meet some people? I want to sell my bracelets."

That one sentence was already a clue. Most kids would have said, "Help me sell these," or "Take me around so I can sell my bracelets."

Not Lauren.

She wanted to meet people. Selling was almost secondary. Connection came first.

"Connection isn't a technique; it is a human truth."

I didn't know it then, but that distinction would become one of the most important lessons of all.

The Bracelets That Meant More Than They Cost

Let me be clear about these bracelets. They were not pieces of fine jewelry. They were simple acrylic beads, hearts, butterflies, and stars, strung together with all the love and creativity a child can put into something she makes by hand. Materially, each bracelet probably cost less than twenty-five cents.

But to Lauren, they were priceless.

Her description said it all:

"I put love, energy, and power in every bead."

That wasn't a sales pitch. She wasn't trying to be clever. She genuinely believed it. The beads might have been plastic, but the meaning behind them was real.

And at ten dollars each, the bracelets weren't cheap. But price is only a barrier when value isn't clear or when the offer isn't made with confidence and genuine intent.

Lauren never had those problems.

Becoming Her "Artificial Intelligence"

Lauren could walk just fine, but because she is blind, she couldn't see who we were approaching. She held onto my elbow as we made our way among the blankets and umbrellas. She relied on me to be her eyes.

"Dad, who's there?" she would ask as we neared each blanket.

I would look ahead and say something like, "A man with his wife and daughter," or "Young couple," or "Group of kids."

Every time, she would respond,

"I got it, Dad."

Years later, I realized something profound.

In those small interactions, I was serving as her artificial intelligence. I was giving her the context she couldn't gather herself, the same way AI gives salespeople insights into their customers today.

I could tell her who we were approaching, but how she connected with them, that part was all her.

And that is the part that matters most.

Lauren's Perfect Invitation

When we reached a blanket, I didn't speak. I didn't prompt her. I simply stood beside her while she did something most adults struggle to do: she connected confidently and warmly.

She smiled, even though she couldn't see their faces, and delivered her now legendary script:

"Hi, my name is Lauren. I make these bead bracelets. There are stars, butterflies, and hearts, and I put love, energy, and power in every bead. They are ten dollars each. How many would you like?"

Notice something crucial.

She didn't ask, "Would you like one?" She didn't ask, "Are you interested?" She didn't ask, "Can I show you these?"

She asked: **How many would you like?**

She didn't push. She didn't pressure. She simply invited.

"People don't respond to pressure; they respond to invitation."

That is a presumptive invitation, friendly, confident, non-pushy, and extremely effective.

The door to "no" was always open, but it wasn't the option she led with. She gave people freedom, but she guided the frame. And because she wasn't afraid of the one answer most sellers dread, she rarely heard it.

That is the power of invitation.

The Curiosity That Created Connection

After her introduction, she didn't rush the sale. Lauren was genuinely curious about people. She wanted to know:

Are you married?

How long?

Do you have kids?

Are you a boyfriend or a girlfriend?

Where are you from?

She wasn't performing a rapport-building technique, she was simply being who she was, a young girl who loved meeting people.

People felt that. Warmth disarms, curiosity opens people up, and authenticity builds connection faster than any scripted question could.

Once people felt that connection, saying yes was the most natural next step.

Lauren never tried to convert anyone; people converted themselves.

She connected, she conveyed value through sincerity, and people chose.

That is what conversion means in Invitational Selling™.

Fifteen Minutes, $85, Zero Pressure

Lauren sold her entire bag of bracelets in about fifteen minutes, and earned $85

on a beach, in July, with no table, no banner, and no signs.

She simply connected with people, conveyed her value, and they converted themselves into happy customers.

Meanwhile, an hour and a half later, Christopher returned from the boardwalk exhausted, frustrated, and holding a dollar and fifty cents in profit.

He had worked hard, but he was in the wrong environment with the wrong approach and no connection.

Lauren, without any sales training, had created a completely different experience.

What She Did with the Money

Lauren wasn't thinking about profit. Whenever she made money, she often used it to buy more beads so she could meet more people. Other times, she donated part of her earnings to causes like Make-A-Wish.

Later that day, she used some of her money to buy ice cream for all her cousins.

For her, selling wasn't about the transaction; it was about connection, generosity, and joy.

People could feel that.

"Selling isn't about the transaction; it's about the connection."

Handling "No" With Grace

Of course, some people said no. They didn't have cash or weren't buying anything that day. When that happened, Lauren's face would fall for just a moment. She genuinely wanted them to have a bracelet.

Then she would brighten and say:

"Well, you should have one anyway."

She would hand them a bracelet for free.

No pressure, no guilt, no attachment, just kindness.

And those moments often meant the most. Some came back later to buy more. Some told friends. Some simply walked away smiling.

Connection outperforms persuasion every time.

The Lessons Hidden in Plain Sight

That day taught me more about selling and leadership than most adults learn in their entire careers.

Here is what Lauren demonstrated, without even knowing it:

- Connection begins with a genuine hello

- Curiosity builds instant rapport because people love to be seen and understood

- Confidence comes from believing in the value you bring, not performing a script

- Clarity always beats cleverness

- Conveying unique value comes from meaning, not materials

- Invitation outperforms persuasion every time

- Generosity builds trust, loyalty, and long-term relationships

- "No" is not rejection; it is information and often a beginning

The Realization That Changed Everything

Watching Lauren that day made something click that had never fully clicked before.

People don't respond to pressure; they respond to invitation.

I gave her context, I described who we were approaching, and I told her what was coming next.

The bracelets didn't sell because they were beautiful, they sold because the interaction was.

"The bracelet wasn't the offer, the interaction was."

That day on the beach didn't just make Lauren $85, it reshaped the way I understood selling and influence.

It showed me that the most powerful "AI" in sales isn't artificial intelligence, it is Authentic Invitation.

In the next chapter, we will explore the core premise of Invitational Selling™ and why the old persuasion model is rapidly breaking down in today's world.

Connection comes first, then value, then invitation.

Let's dig in.

Key Takeaways:

- Connection always comes first because people open up when they feel seen and acknowledged.

- Curiosity builds trust faster than any technique because it shows you care.

- Convey value through meaning because people respond to sincerity more than features.

- Confidence creates clarity, and when you believe in your value others do too.

- Conversion is never forced because people choose when it feels human and honest.

- Generosity strengthens relationships and creates moments people remember.

- "No" is not rejection, it is information and often an invitation to understand.

- "How many would you like?" is the purest expression of Connect → Convey → Covert™ in action.

CHAPTER 2
Why Persuasion Fails and Invitation Wins
The Core of Invitational Selling™

We've all been there. You are in a normal conversation, everything feels fine, and then suddenly you sense that subtle shift, the moment the other person starts selling at you instead of selling for you.

It is jarring.

It is uncomfortable.

And it instantly changes the way your brain processes the interaction.

At that moment, your inside voice kicks in like the robot from the sci-fi show *Lost in Space*, waving its arms and shouting, "Danger, Will Robinson, danger!"

We might smile or nod politely, but mentally we begin planning our escape. We disconnect. We stop listening. We protect ourselves. And we do all of this automatically.

Not because we are rude.

Not because we don't like the person.

And not even because we don't need what they are offering.

We shut down because our brain does something very predictable when it senses pressure.

This reaction is exactly why persuasion-based selling is losing effectiveness in today's world and why Invitational Selling™ is becoming essential.

"The moment pressure enters a conversation, connection begins to disappear."

Why Persuasion Is Outdated

There was a time when persuasion worked. It was built for a world that had:

- Very little noise

- Limited choices

- Slower decision cycles

- Fewer sources of information

Salespeople controlled the message. Buyers relied on them for expertise. The salesperson held the power and the information.

That world no longer exists.

Today's buyers have:

- Unlimited access to data

- Endless alternatives

- Instant comparison tools

- Constant digital overload

- Less tolerance for manipulation than eve

Add AI-generated messaging to the mix, and everything begins to sound the same. Most sales communication today lacks differentiation, humanity, and clarity.

Here is the real shift:

Persuasion assumes the seller is in control.

Today, the buyer is in control.

Persuasion tries to push a decision.

Invitation creates room for a decision.

The Science Behind Autonomy and Why Pressure Backfires

The reason persuasion fails isn't just a feeling. It is rooted in neuroscience.

When people feel pressured, three predictable things happen:

1. **The Amygdala Activates the Threat Response**

   Research suggests the brain's threat-detection system becomes more active when people feel pressured. The brain interprets pressure as danger. Even subtle pressure can create resistance, defensiveness, and mental narrowing.

2. **Autonomy Becomes the Priority**

   Research in Self-Determination Theory suggests people become more open, engaged, and motivated when they feel a sense of choice and control. When autonomy feels threatened, people pull away.

3. **Connection Releases Serotonin, Creating Comfort**

   Connection isn't just emotional; it is chemical. When people feel understood and respected, the brain releases serotonin, which promotes:

- Comfort

- Emotional stability

- Openness

- Trust

This is why connection always precedes influence.

"Autonomy activates commitment, pressure destroys it."

A Quick Word On Brain Chemistry (Without Going "Sciency")

There is ample research on how our hormones influence trust, connection, bonding, tension, and anxiety. I am not going to go "sciency" here, but I want one thing to be clear:

The way we communicate changes the way people feel.

The way people feel changes the way they decide.

Communication that creates connection releases chemicals that help people feel open, relaxed, and receptive.

Communication that creates pressure activates protection.

Biology is on the side of invitational communication.

A Lesson That Changed How I See Human Decisions

Early in my career, long before I became a speaker or worked with leaders and organizations, I learned a powerful lesson about autonomy while working with patients in my chiropractic practice.

What I discovered was simple but profound: **When people feel ownership of a decision, they follow through. When they feel directed, they resist.**

That experience quietly shaped everything I teach today. I'll unpack that lesson in detail later in the book, but for now, understand this, **pressure doesn't fail because people are stubborn, it fails because autonomy matters.**

"Clarity empowers people. Choice transforms them."

That experience became one of the foundational truths of Invitational Selling™:

- Clarity empowers

- Autonomy activates commitment

- People walk the path they choose more confidently than the path they are pushed toward

People aren't resistant by nature. They are resistant when they feel controlled.

This is why invitation consistently outperforms persuasion.

Why Invitation Works Better Than Persuasion

Invitation works because it aligns with how people are wired.

When you invite instead of persuade:

- The brain relaxes

- Resistance drops

- Curiosity increases

- Trust rises

- Communication becomes easier

- The relationship feels safer

Here is something important to understand.

Even though it leaves the decisions up to others, Invitational Selling™ is not passive, weak, or vague.

It is intentional.

It is confident.

It is clear.

It removes pressure so the other person can lean in instead of pull back.

It is better to be clear than clever.

Persuasion often hides behind clever phrases.

Invitation is built on clarity.

Lauren wasn't clever.

She was clear.

And clarity changed everything.

Connection Before Conversion

Connection is no longer optional.

It is essential.

People don't buy because of a script.

They buy because of:

- Presence

- Intent

- Energy

- Trust

Connection creates safety. Safety leads to openness. Openness leads to willingness.

If you skip connection and go straight to convincing, you create resistance. If you start with connection, every next step becomes easier.

Invitational Selling™ begins with the relationship, not the pitch.

"Connection creates the conditions where invitation can succeed."

Where AI Fits into This New Era of Selling

Artificial intelligence can:

- Analyze patterns

- Predict buying behavior

- Personalize messages

- Prepare insights

- Help you understand your audience

When preparing for sales or leadership conversations, AI can give you insight into who you are approaching, much like I did for Lauren when she held my elbow on the beach.

But AI cannot:

- Build trust

- Create emotional safety

- Read the room

- Show genuine curiosity

- Offer warmth

- Make someone feel valued

- Deliver a sincere invitation

AI informs the interaction.

Humans transform the interaction.

The real competitive edge isn't choosing between AI and authenticity; it is combining them.

AI for information.

You for invitation.

That is a strategic advantage most organizations never develop.

The Mindset Shift That Changes Everything

Invitational Selling™ begins with a simple shift:

Your job isn't to convince people.

Your job is to invite them.

When you internalize that shift:

- Confidence rises

- Anxiety drops

- Conversations feel natural

- Pressure disappears

- People open up

- Decisions come easier

You stop sounding like someone who wants something, and start sounding like someone who *offers something*.

That is influence.

Clarity, Value, and the Next Step

Every successful invitation follows a simple structure:

If you build rapport, you earn attention. If you communicate and convey your value clearly, you earn consideration.

If you extend a genuine invitation, you earn action.

Persuasion tries to force the third step before earning the first two.

Invitation guides people through the process naturally.

Now that you understand the core premise behind Invitational Selling™, let's look at the framework that makes it so effective.

Invitational Selling™ is built on three pillars:

- Build genuine rapport

- Communicate unique value

- Invite the next step

Master these three skills, and you will communicate with more clarity, confidence, and impact than ever before.

Let's begin with Pillar One: Building Genuine Rapport.

Key Takeaways:

- Persuasion creates resistance, while invitation creates openness.

- Pressure shuts down decision-making because it threatens autonomy.

- Invitation signals respect, safety, and shared control.

- The human brain responds far better to connection than to coercion.

- People trust and engage more deeply when they do not feel pushed.

- Invitational Selling™ replaces force with clarity, confidence, and respect.

- This model works today because people instantly detect traditional sales pressure.

- The person who invites becomes the person who is trusted.

CHAPTER 3

The Three Pillars
of Invitational Selling

Why Every Successful Conversation
Follows the Same Structure

If you've ever been stuck in a conversation where someone starts talking, and you are not sure what they are talking about, or why they are talking about it, or how on earth you got pulled into it, you know what a wandering conversation feels like.

It starts with something innocent like, "You know, this reminds me of a thing my uncle did," and suddenly you are hearing about a 1998 fishing trip, the one that happened right after he bought a used pickup truck that he later traded for a motorcycle, which he does not even have anymore because his neighbor borrowed it and never returned it. By the time he gets to the point, you have forgotten what the original conversation was about in the first place.

It is painful, it is disorienting, and most of all, it makes you want to quietly back away and save yourself.

A wandering conversation makes the listener feel lost.

A purposeful conversation makes the listener feel safe.

That difference, wandering versus purposeful, is exactly why the structure of Invitational Selling™ matters so much.

When you understand the structure, your communication becomes intuitive, natural, and effective. When you do not, even the best intentions can come across as confusing, overwhelming, or worse, like pressure.

"Purposeful conversations make people feel safe, understood, and ready to engage."

The Structure Lauren Revealed Without Knowing It

Back on that hot July beach, Lauren had no idea she was demonstrating a communication method many adults never master.

But she was.

She naturally followed the same three pillars this chapter is about. She built rapport through curiosity, she conveyed meaningful value with clarity, and she invited without pressure by asking, "How many would you like?"

She was not trained, she was not scripted, she was simply authentic.

And authenticity follows a very simple structure.

The Three Pillars of Invitational Selling

And How They Map to Connect, Convey, Convert

Every effective sales conversation, and honestly every effective human conversation, follows the same foundational sequence.

Pillar 1: Connect — Build Genuine Rapport

Connection before conversation.

Pillar 2: Convey — Communicate Unique Value

Clarity before complexity.

Pillar 3: Convert — Invite the Next Step, Not Pressure

Freedom before force.

Whether you are selling a product, a service, an idea, or even yourself, these three pillars guide the interaction, so it feels natural, respectful, and human.

Skip one and things fall apart quickly.

"Connect, Convey, Convert is not a tactic, it is the natural rhythm of human decision-making."

Why Pillar 1 Comes First

Rapport Before Anything Else (CONNECT)

Rapport is the emotional foundation of influence. Without it, nothing else sticks.

People do not listen until they feel connected.

People do not open up until they feel safe.

People do not make decisions until they feel understood.

Unfortunately, too many sales methods, and leadership strategies, avoid connection by burying them under layers of tactics and scripts.

Without rapport, everything else feels like persuasion or pressure.

Rapport is not small talk, it is not forced enthusiasm, it is not pretending to care to get the sale. *Genuine rapport is created through curiosity, presence, connection, and respect.* It tells the other person's brain, "You are safe here," which opens the door to everything that follows.

Rapport is the Connect stage in action.

Why Pillar 2 Matters

Communicating Unique Value Clearly (CONVEY)

Once rapport is established, people are ready for clarity. Not cleverness, not performance, not scripts. Clarity.

People want to know who you are, what you offer, why it matters, how it helps them, and why it is different. They want the information in a way that is easy to understand and impossible to misinterpret.

Clarity builds confidence.

Confusion kills momentum.

Lauren's bracelets were not expensive, but her description was priceless because it was simple, meaningful, and honest.

"I put love, energy, and power in every bead."

No jargon, no hype, just genuine value.

That is what people respond to, and that is the essence of Convey.

Why Pillar 3 Is the Game-Changer

Invitation Over Persuasion (CONVERT)

Once rapport is built and value is communicated, the final pillar is what turns a conversation into a decision.

Inviting the next step without pressure.

An invitation respects autonomy. It communicates, "I believe this can help you, and I would love for you to take the next step, but the choice is yours."

A pressured pitch communicates, "I need you to say yes, and I am going to push until you do."

One way opens people up. The other one shuts them down.

And even though we are only up to chapter 3, you don't need me to tell you which is which because we all innately understand this.

Invitation is built on confidence, generosity, clarity, and respect for the other person's agency.

Persuasion tries to force movement, invitation creates space for movement.

This is why Lauren's question, "How many would you like?" was so effective. It was not pushy, it was not manipulative, it simply offered a clear next step inside a comfortable relationship.

That is the heart of Convert, an invitation that empowers the other person rather than cornering them.

How the Three Pillars Work Together

The pillars are not random, they are sequential, and they reinforce each other.

Here is how they flow.

Connect - Rapport earns attention

People listen because they trust you.

Convey - Value earns consideration

People stay engaged because they understand you.

Convert - Invitation earns action

People decide because they feel respected by you, and converting happens through invitation, not pressure or persuasion.

When you follow this sequence, conversations unfold naturally. When you skip steps, everything feels harder.

This framework ensures the interaction is human, purposeful, and easy for the other person to navigate.

"Rapport earns attention. Value earns consideration. Invitation earns action."

The Cost of Skipping a Pillar

Skipping rapport makes the conversation feel transactional.

Skipping value makes the message feel confusing.

Skipping the invitation leaves the other person unsure of what to do next.

People want clarity, people want guidance, people want the freedom to choose, not the pressure to comply.

The three pillars ensure the person you are speaking with feels respected, understood, and empowered.

A Simple Model to Remember

Think of the three pillars as a path.

Rapport, Value, Invitation = Connect, Convey, Convert.

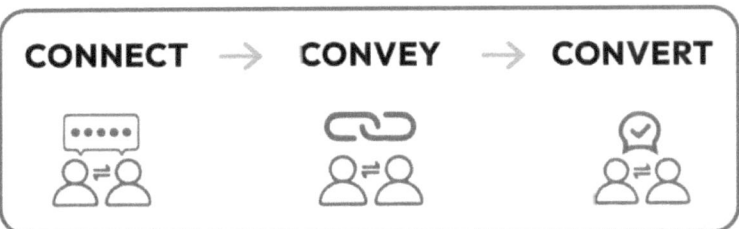

It reflects a natural, human sequence. It is not a tactic, it is not a script, it is not manipulation. It is simply the way people want you to communicate with them.

When you follow this path, influence becomes easier, conversations become lighter, and results become more consistent.

Now that you know the three pillars, we begin with the first and most essential one.

Rapport is not a warm-up.

It is the moment that determines everything that follows.

Key Takeaways:

- Rapport earns attention.

- Value clarity earns consideration.

- Invitation earns action.

- Connect, Convey, Convert is the structure underneath every successful conversation.

- Most sales break down because people skip the first two pillars.

- When you honor autonomy, you amplify influence.

CHAPTER 4

Build Genuine Rapport

Connection Before Conversation

There are few things more uncomfortable than someone trying way too hard to "build rapport." You know the moment. You sit down for a meeting, shake hands, and before you can even put your coffee down, the other person launches in with something like, "So … how about that weather we're having, huh? Crazy, right? I mean, rain in the spring! Who could have guessed?"

Or they hit you with the classic triple stack.

"Where are you from? Oh, my cousin's roommate's dentist lives there. Small world, right?"

Or my personal favorite, the accidental interrogation.

"How was your weekend? What did you do? Where did you go? Who did you see? Did you have fun? Why not? Are you okay?"

By the time they are done "connecting," you feel less like you're in a conversation and more like you survived a pop quiz you didn't study for.

Most people have no idea how to build rapport. And it shows.

Forced rapport is awkward,

Rushed rapport is uncomfortable,

Fake rapport is painful.

But genuine rapport, the kind that makes people relax, open up, and trust you, is simple.

It is not about charm, jokes, flattery, or weather commentary. It is not about proving you are interesting or impressive. And it is definitely not about pretending to care when you actually just want to get to your pitch.

Rapport, at its core, is emotional safety.

It is the feeling people get when they sense, "I am safe here. I can be myself. And this person actually sees me."

That feeling unlocks everything that follows.

And this matters now more than ever because rapport is the essence of Connecting in the Connect, Convey, Convert™ framework. Without connection, nothing else works.

"Rapport is emotional safety, not small talk."

Why Rapport Comes First

Rapport is not a warm-up to the conversation. It is the foundation of the conversation.

Without it, people:

- Do not listen

- Do not trust

- Do not open up

- Do not share what matters

- Do not take action

And it is not because they are difficult. It is because the brain has a built-in safety system that decides, within seconds, whether a conversation feels safe or threatening.

When people feel pressured, that safety system activates and triggers the exact response you don't want. That includes resistance, shutdown, and the rapid erosion of trust.

When people feel connection, the brain shifts into states associated with comfort and openness, the states required for trust, clarity, and collaboration.

Rapport lowers resistance before resistance ever has a chance to show up.

This is exactly why Lauren's curiosity worked so well on the beach. She didn't try to build rapport. She simply connected with people. She made them feel seen. Safety, not strategy, opened the door to influence.

Forced Rapport Versus Genuine Rapport

You can feel the difference immediately.

Forced rapport feels like:

- Exaggerated friendliness

- Scripted "How are you?" questions no one means

- Awkward mirroring

- Complimenting someone's tie or scarf like it is a rare museum piece

- Pretending to care about something you don't

- Trying too hard to "relate" Forced rapport creates tension, not connection.

Genuine rapport feels like:

- Presence

- Curiosity

- Interest

- Warmth

- Listening

- Steady, calm energy

Genuine rapport is not something you do. It is something you create.

Curiosity, The Fastest Path to Connection

If there is one rapport skill that outperforms all others, it is curiosity.

Curiosity disarms.

Curiosity relaxes.

Curiosity shows care.

Curiosity makes the other person feel valued.

People love talking about their lives, goals, challenges, wins, frustrations, and hopes. When you ask a real question, a meaningful question, you activate their desire to share.

Especially, and this is critical, when you truly care about the response.

Questions like:

- "What has your focus these days?"

- "What are you excited about right now?"

- "What is something you are working toward?"

Curiosity tells someone, "I see you, I care, and this moment is about you."

That simple shift changes everything.

But asking the right question is only half the equation. Being fully present for the answer is what creates safety.

"Curiosity is the fastest path to connection."

Presence as a Rapport Skill

Presence is the secret ingredient that makes rapport feel authentic.

Presence means:

- You are not rushing

- You are not distracted

- You are not rehearsing your next line

- You are not forcing the conversation forward

- You are truly listening

People can feel presence before a single word is spoken. They feel it in your tone, your pacing, your eye contact, and your energy.

Presence replaces pressure.

Presence feels safe.

Presence builds rapport without effort.

And sometimes presence, and the emotional safety it creates, leads to moments that change everything.

A Moment of Emotional Safety That Changed Everything

Stacey's Story

A few years ago, I worked with an estate planning attorney named Stacey, a sharp and compassionate professional from Canada who had been bullied as a child. She came to one of my three-day events, a workshop that combines the Invitational Selling™ philosophy with speaking from the stage, because she wanted to communicate with more confidence and clarity as a way to grow her Law Firm.

During the workshop, we teach something essential:

Your unique story, your "why," belongs at the very beginning of your presentation.

It builds rapport.

It humanizes.

It creates emotional safety.

It lets people feel who you are before you tell them what you do.

Stacey understood the concept.

She believed in it when she watched others use it.

She saw its power.

A week after completing the program, Stacy delivered a community seminar. It was the first in a four-part educational series. She was the organizer, and she spoke first. She delivered her content clearly and confidently.

But when it came time for her to share her Differentiating Story™, she froze.

She worried that telling people she had been bullied would make her look weak or less credible as a lawyer. So despite everything she learned, she left her story out of her presentation entirely.

Then, during the Q&A Session at the end, someone raised their hand and asked the question she had silently hoped would never come:

"Why do you do this work?"

In that instant, she realized she had avoided the very piece of her message that would have mattered most. Her differentiating story.

She took a breath.

She remembered the training.

And she decided to tell the truth.

She shared that she had been bullied growing up, and that it shaped her into someone who refuses to let fear or intimidation damage families during already difficult times. She explained that her law firm exists to protect relationships, reduce conflict, and prevent emotional harm.

When she finished, the room went silent.

Then the audience began to clap.

And they kept clapping.

She later told me she was so surprised she curtsied, something she had not done since childhood.

After the seminar, people lined up to talk with her. One attendee emailed her saying:

"Everyone fell in love with you at that moment. Your purpose sets you apart from every estate specialist."

That night, she booked six new clients.

Three more appointments came in the following week.

But the real transformation wasn't the business she earned; it was the realization that the story she was most afraid to share was the story that created the deepest trust.

"People don't respond to perfection; they respond to sincerity."

People don't respond to perfection. They respond to sincerity, and sincerity is what makes every meaningful invitation possible. It opens the door to influence without pressure, persuasion, or convincing. It is the heart of Invitational Selling™.

Micro-Behaviors That Build Rapport Instantly

These small behaviors are subtle but powerful:

- A genuine, warm greeting

- Saying someone's name naturally

- Asking a simple opening question that shows interest

- Matching their energy level without mimicking

- Letting people finish their thoughts

- Responding to what they actually said, not what you expected

These moments communicate respect,

and respect creates rapport.

Rapport Breakers That Create Instant Disconnection

Rapport can be built quickly, but it can be broken even quicker.

Common rapport breakers include:

- Interrupting

- Talking too fast

- Jumping straight into your agenda

- Sounding scripted

- Being overly cheerful or overly serious

- Asking fake "rapport questions" you don't care about

Once rapport breaks, the conversation becomes heavier, and it takes more work to recover.

Why People Resist Rapport When They Need It Most

People often avoid rapport for one of three reasons:

They think it takes too long

They are afraid it will feel fake

They think it is unprofessional

None of these are true.

Genuine rapport doesn't take long.

Genuine rapport doesn't feel fake.

Genuine rapport isn't unprofessional.

Genuine rapport is respectful.

It is the permission to begin the conversation.

Rapport Protects Autonomy

People open up when they do not feel controlled. Genuine rapport honors autonomy by allowing people to share at their own pace and in their own way. When someone feels free rather than steered, they lean toward openness instead of resistance.

This is why rapport creates such a strong foundation, not just for the conversation, but for the invitation that will eventually follow.

Building Rapport at Scale, Teams, Leaders, and Organizations

Rapport is not just a sales skill.

It is a leadership skill.

A culture-building skill.

A communication skill.

Teams that build rapport:

- Communicate more clearly

- Avoid unnecessary conflict

- Collaborate more easily

- Solve problems faster

- Retain talent longer

Across the organizations I have worked with, the biggest breakthroughs rarely came from learning better "scripts."

They came from leaders who mastered the art of creating conversations where people felt safe, respected, and truly heard.

Rapport is the starting point for every high-performing culture.

A Simple Framework for Building Rapport

You can build rapport quickly and naturally by following four simple steps:

Connection

Acknowledge the human being in front of you.

Curiosity

Ask one meaningful question that shows interest.

Context

Let them share what matters to them, and listen fully.

Caring

Respond in a way that shows you heard them.

This may seem simple, but never underestimate its power.

Where We Go Next

Once rapport opens the door and creates emotional safety,

the next step is to convey your unique value with clarity.

People will only consider your offer when they understand it,

believe it, and feel the meaning behind it.

In the next chapter, we will explore how to communicate value in a way that is simple, powerful, and impossible to misunderstand.

"Rapport makes every future invitation possible."

Key Takeaways:

- Rapport is emotional safety, not small talk.

- Rapport is the essence of Connect in the Connect, Convey, Convert model.

- Curiosity is the fastest path to connection.

- Presence communicates respect more than any technique.

- People open up when they feel seen, heard, and understood.

- Rapport is not a step; it is the foundation that makes every future invitation meaningful.

CHAPTER 5

Convey And Communicate Your Unique Value

Clarity Before Complexity

Most people think they are clear when they communicate, but they're not.

If you have ever asked someone, "So what do you do?" and they responded with a sentence so long, so tangled, and so buzzword-loaded that it sounded like the back of a shampoo bottle, you know what I mean.

Perhaps they said something like:

"We provide an omni-channel, synergistically aligned engagement ecosystem that leverages paradigm-shifting solutions across multiple verticals."

Great.

Fantastic.

What does that mean?

When people talk like this, you do not lean in, you lean back.

Confusing communication does not impress people, it exhausts them.

Your unique value should feel simple, obvious, and meaningful, not confusing, clever, or complicated.

Conveying your value is the second pillar of Invitational Selling, and it is essential for success in every sales and leadership situation.

Value Is Not What You Sell, It Is What They Feel

Most people think the "value" of what they offer is the product, the service, or the feature.

It is not.

Value is emotional, value is personal, value is meaning.

Lauren understood this without ever being taught.

Those bracelets she sold on the beach were made from acrylic beads that maybe cost twenty-five cents. They were simple, common, replaceable, but people were not buying the beads.

They were buying what Lauren put into them.

Love,

Energy,

Power.

Those were her words, that was her value.

The materials were cheap, the meaning was priceless.

People bought the feeling she created, not the object she handed them.

"Your value is not the thing; it is the meaning behind the thing."

The same is true for your business. Your value is not the thing; it is the meaning you attach to the thing.

When you understand this, your entire communication style changes.

Why Clarity Wins Over Cleverness

People often try to sound impressive or highly intelligent when explaining their value. They complicate the message, add unnecessary language, and create what I call value fog.

"If your message makes them work, they won't."

Cleverness hides meaning, clarity reveals value.

If someone needs a translator to understand what you do, you are not communicating value; you are creating confusion.

Here's another example of "clever" communication that sounds impressive but means absolutely nothing:

"We empower organizations to unlock transformative bandwidth by operationalizing next-generation efficiencies that align cross-functional relevance."

If you have to decode it like hieroglyphics, it is not valuable, it is noise.

Clear communication respects the listener; clever communication confuses them.

The Curse of Knowledge

Smart people are the worst!

I say this lovingly… but they're still the worst.

It is not intentional. They simply assume everyone else understands what they understand.

I work with doctors, attorneys, engineers, CEOs, and highly educated professionals every day. Brilliant people. Yet many explain things at the level they understand them, not at the level their clients need them to.

Here is the newsflash.

They do not understand what you are talking about. And even if they pretend to, their brain is struggling to keep up.

Here is what actually happens inside the listener's mind.

You are explaining something with technical language, thinking it shows expertise, but here is what their brain experiences:

Confusion

→ Frustration

→ "I feel stupid"

→ "You made me feel stupid"

→ "I do not like you"

→ "I am not doing business with you or I'm not going to listen to you"

People do not buy from, or follow, someone who makes them feel stupid.

Now, I could have opened this entire section by saying that what you are triggering is something Leon Festinger called cognitive dissonance, but…

I did not want to make you feel stupid.

You are welcome.

This is why clarity matters more than cleverness. It is also why Lauren's Differentiating Story worked so beautifully. She kept everything simple, heartfelt, and human.

Translate Features into Real Benefits

Before we get into examples, let me be clear about this very important fact.

Nobody cares about what you do or what you sell. They care about what it does for them.

What outcome does it create?

What problem does it solve?

What positive change does it make in their life?

This is the difference between features and benefits.

Many of my clients mistakenly believe that listing more features makes their offer more valuable. They confuse volume with value, and nothing could be further from the truth.

Your customers want to know one thing:

What's in it for me?

Their brain is always scanning for one question:

"Does this make my life easier, better, safer, faster, simpler, or less annoying?"

If you cannot answer that, you lose them.

Remember this:

The feature is "what it is" and the benefit is "what it does" for your client.

For example:

"Fast processing" = feature

"Saves you hours every week" = benefit

"People do not buy features; they buy what the features do for them."

Share Who You Are Before What You Sell

"No one has ever said, 'Your product confuses me, but what a delightful human you are, here is my credit card.'"

But they have said:

"I feel good with you ... tell me more."

Connection first, always.

Your identity, your credibility, your experience, and your story all fuel your value. This is why your Differentiating Story matters.

Lauren did not talk about beads. She talked about what she put into them.

Your story does the same thing.

People connect with the human behind the offer. When they understand *your why*, they listen to *your what* with more openness and trust.

The Power of Simple, Human Language

You do not influence people by being complex. You influence them by being clear.

Research consistently shows that the most effective communication is written at a sixth to eighth grade reading level. This is not about dumbing down, it is about removing friction.

Clear language is respectful, complicated language is selfish.

"Clear language is respectful, complicated language is selfish."

Here is something I tell my clients all the time.

"If you have to explain what the name of your product or program means after you say it, it is not a good name. Skip the name and tell me what it means."

Micro Skills That Help You Communicate Unique Value

These small shifts create major clarity.

- Speak in headlines before details.

- Use one idea per sentence.

- Lead with outcomes, not descriptions.

- Use concrete examples.

- Avoid jargon.

- Be specific

- Use real words.

- Remove filler.

- Shorten sentences for impact.

Tiny changes, huge difference.

What People Really Want to Know

When you communicate your value, people are subconsciously listening for four things.

- Do you understand me?

- Do you care about me?

- Can you help me?

- Why should I trust you?

If your message answers these questions with clarity and simplicity, people become more open, more engaged, and more willing to take the next step.

A Simple Framework for Communicating Value

You can communicate value quickly and clearly with this four-step formula.

1. **State the value simply.**

2. **Explain why it matters.**

3. **Show how it helps them.**

4. **Give a real example.**

This removes confusion, builds trust, and makes your message easy to absorb.

When people clearly understand the value you bring, the next step becomes simple. You extend a clean, confident, respectful invitation.

In the next chapter, we will explore how to invite people into action without pressure, and how a well framed invitation becomes one of the most powerful tools in your communication toolbox.

Key Takeaways:

- If people cannot repeat your value, they cannot buy it.

- Clarity beats cleverness every time.

- Your differentiating story shows who you are behind what you sell.

- Value is emotional before it is logical.

- The simpler your value is to understand, the easier it is to say yes.

CHAPTER 6

Invitation, Not Pressure

Why Autonomy Creates Better Decisions

Most people do not dislike sales.

They dislike pressure.

They dislike the feeling of being pushed, cornered, or "sold at," instead of being understood, respected, and invited.

When you understand this, Invitational Selling™ becomes the most natural form of communication on the planet. Because instead of forcing a decision, you create a space where the decision becomes easy.

Let's begin with a truth most people never admit out loud:

People love to say yes.

They just hate feeling forced into it.

When people feel connected to you, pressure naturally dissolves. Connection creates safety, safety creates openness, and openness is the doorway to every meaningful conversation.

"Pressure reduces trust, connection reduces pressure,."

Pressure Shrinks the Brain, Autonomy Expands It

Earlier in the book, we talked about how pressure can flip the brain's internal alarm system into overdrive. When someone feels pushed, their brain may immediately trigger a threat response. When that happens, their "inside voice" starts warning them that something is off.

But here is the important part. There is real research suggesting that when people feel autonomy, the brain shifts into a more open, receptive state.

This comes from what psychologists Edward Deci and Richard Ryan describe as Self Determination Theory, which suggests that humans tend to be more motivated when they experience three things:

- Autonomy

- Competence

- Relatedness

To put it simply:

- When People Feel They Have a Choice, They Open Up

- When They Feel Respected, They Listen

- When They Feel Understood, They Act

Autonomy lowers defensiveness.

Autonomy increases intrinsic motivation.

Invitations create autonomy.

Pressure destroys it.

Connection opens the mind.

Autonomy opens the heart.

And once someone feels safe, you can convey value without resistance.

"Autonomy turns clarity into action."

Invitations Are Respectful, Clear, and Honest

Invitational Selling™ is built on a simple belief:

People make better decisions when they do not feel coerced.

A clear invitation:

- Respects their intelligence

- Honors their autonomy

- Simplifies their decision

- Increases their comfort

- Reduces tension

- Accelerates action

Pressure-based selling, on the other hand, makes the buyer feel *controlled* instead of *considered.*

An invitation says, "Here's something that might help. You decide."

Pressure says, "You need to do this. Now."

When you connect first and convey value simply, conversion becomes a natural next step, not an outcome you force, but an outcome they choose.

Lauren's Lesson: The Genius of an Assumed Yes

Lauren never pressured anyone on the beach, but she did something incredibly effective without knowing it.

She invited action without limiting it.

She never asked, "Would you like one?"

She always asked, "How many would you like?"

This language does two brilliant things:

- It presumes interest without forcing it

- It frames the decision around quantity instead of permission

Could someone still say no?

Of course.

But overwhelmingly, they didn't.

Why?

Because her question signaled confidence, clarity, and sincerity. It made taking action feel simple and natural.

And because she began with genuine connection, smiling, engaging, making people feel seen, her invitation felt natural, not intrusive.

"Assumed yes works because it honors the relationship, not the script."

The Four Elements of a Powerful Invitation

A great invitation does not need to be long. It needs to be:

- Clear

- Confident

- Respectful

- Open

Examples:

"Based on what you shared, it sounds like this program could help you. If you'd like, we can schedule a quick call to talk it through."

"I think this could be a strong fit for your team. Want to take the next step and explore it?"

"If it makes sense, the next option is to look at the proposal. Would you like me to send it?"

And here is a humble, highly effective version:

"I'm not sure if this is right for you, but we have something you might be interested in."

This line lowers resistance instantly. It gives the listener room to move toward the offer without feeling nudged into it.

The Language of Invitations Vs. The Language of Pressure

Pressure Language

- You need to do this

- This offer expires in five minutes

- If you don't act now, you'll fall behind

- You really should buy this

- You'd be crazy not to

Invitation Language

- If you feel this would help, here's the next step

- When you're ready, here are your options

- If it makes sense, we can look at this together

- You decide what fits best

- I'm here when you're ready

Invitations create space.

Pressure creates pushback.

And pushback kills trust.

Why Invitations Reduce Buyer's Remorse

There is another major advantage to Invitational Selling™ that most people overlook:

It eliminates buyer's remorse.

When people make decisions under pressure, the decision feels artificial. They did not choose freely. They chose because of tension, urgency, or fear. And when that pressure disappears, so does their confidence.

This is why pressured buyers:

- Cancel more

- Request refunds

- Return products

- Second-guess themselves

- Leave negative reviews

- Avoid future purchases

But when someone says yes because they feel invited, not pushed, something completely different happens.

They feel ownership.

They feel alignment.

They feel good about the decision.

There is no remorse afterward because the decision was theirs.

Clients who feel ownership:

- Are happier with their purchase

- Complain less

- Implement more

- Get better results

- Are far more likely to refer others

Invitational Selling™ improves the experience before, during, and after the decision.

The Chiropractic Lesson That Showed Me the Power of Autonomy

Before I ever taught sales, speaking, or communication, I learned one of my most important lessons about human behavior while working as a chiropractor.

Many of my patients came in with chronic problems, issues requiring extended care to resolve. Often the best path forward was coming in two or three times a week for eight to twelve weeks before reevaluating.

In the early days, I made the classic mistake: I simply told people what they needed.

"You need to come in three times a week for the next two months."

And almost every time, I got pushback.

People resisted.

They felt overwhelmed.

They stopped showing up.

And the ones who quit early rarely got the results they wanted.

It wasn't because the care plan was wrong.

It was because people don't like being told what to do.

So I changed everything.

Instead of giving orders, I invited patients back the next day to review their X rays. First, I showed them what a normal X ray looked like. I explained normal curvature, spacing, and range of motion.

Then I put their X ray next to the normal one.

Instead of telling them the problem, I asked:

"Based on what you see here, what do you think is going on?"

They didn't need medical terminology.

They could see it.

They understood the issue without being pressured into agreement.

By connecting first and conveying the information clearly, I didn't need to convince anyone. The invitation to choose their path forward became the natural moment of conversion.

Only then did I explain:

"People with your condition who want the best results in the shortest amount of time usually come in two to three times a week for eight to twelve weeks before reevaluating."

Then came the most important part.

I asked them:

"What would you like to do?"

And then I stayed quiet.

Almost every time, they chose the care plan I would have recommended. But the difference was profound:

They chose it.

They owned it.

They followed through.

Their attendance improved.

Their progress accelerated.

Their satisfaction increased.

How I Learned the Difference Between Pressure and Invitation

People often ask me how I know all of this to be true.

I know it because I have lived both sides of it.

I have used pressure without realizing the damage it caused, and I have used invitation and watched people step forward with confidence instead of fear.

Early in my career, long before I became a keynote speaker, I was working as a chiropractor. Out of the blue, I was invited to join one of the largest seminar companies in North America as a lead trainer.

The training was intense.

Three full days.

Hours of teaching and coaching.

And multiple sales offers from the stage.

When I began, I struggled with selling. Not because I didn't believe in the programs, but because the way I had never "sold from the stage" before.

So, I studied the top sellers.

They relied on the hard sell.

They pushed.

They bullied.

They manipulated.

They used guilt and fear.

They created artificial scarcity.

And it worked.

So, I studied them and learned to do what they did.

Within a short time, I mastered it too.

I became one of the top sellers in the company.

But it never felt right.

The energy was tense.

The trust evaporated.

And afterward, the cancellations poured in.

That's when it hit me:

For the audience, the hard-sell produced transactions, not decisions.

It created buyers, not believers. It forced action, but it destroyed trust.

For me, it just didn't "feel right."

So, I tried something completely different. I completely revised my approach to selling from the stage.

I began focusing on rapport.

I connected with the audience.

I shared stories.

I conveyed value clearly and honestly.

And then, I simply invited them to take the next step.

No pressure.

No guilt.

No manipulation.

Just a genuine invitation.

"Conversion is the outcome of connection and clarity, not control."

People still stood up and went to the back of the room. But not nearly as many as before.

My "at event" sales numbers plummeted.

It was incredibly disappointing in the moment. I remember thinking I might get fired for poor performance.

In a blink of an eye, I dropped from the top salesperson to near the bottom.

Or, so I thought at the time.

What I had failed to take into consideration in that moment was the cancellation rate. You see, in the seminar industry "at seminar" sales numbers are important, but what matters even more are the 90-day numbers. Those are the numbers that represent remaining sales after all cancellations and changes have been accounted for in the first three months.

The 90-day numbers show how many of the registrations and sales have actually processed and confirmed in the system. In other words, these numbers represent the actual sales that the company realized from the event.

While my "At Event" sales may have been the lowest, the cancellation rates at my programs was also the lowest, by a wide margin.

As a result, my 90-day sales numbers (after cancellations were accounted for) were consistently the highest in the company.

Invitational Selling™ worked, even though I hadn't defined it at the time.

People who enrolled through invitation stayed enrolled.

They didn't second-guess their choice.

They didn't regret their decision.

They bought because they wanted to, not because they were cornered.

Pressure creates buyer's remorse.

Invitation creates lasting change.

That is Invitational Selling™.

Why Invitations Work Better Than Persuasion

Invitational Selling works because it follows a natural human pattern:

Connect, convey, convert.

Persuasion says, "Let me convince you."

Invitation says, "Let me support you."

Persuasion demands.

Invitation empowers.

Persuasion tries to control the outcome.

Invitation opens the door to possibility.

Ironically, invitations lead to more yeses than persuasion and pressure ever will. Not because they manipulate, but because they honor how people make decisions: through autonomy, connection, clarity, and trust.

The Simple Structure of an Effective Invitation

Here is a practical four step framework you can use in almost any situation:

- Reflect what you heard

- Convey the value simply

- Offer the next step

- Return the autonomy

And as I often share with my clients, sales is incredibly simple.

It really boils down to saying three things:

I see you have a problem.

I can help.

What do you want to do?

That's it.

That's sales.

That is Invitational Selling™.

The Emotional Impact of an Invitation

When you offer someone an invitation instead of pressure, something powerful happens:

- They relax

- Their guard drops

- They trust more

- They listen better

- They open up

- They think clearly

- They say yes more often

Because the brain prefers choices, not commands.

Choices signal safety.

Commands signal danger.

Invitational Selling™ creates cooperation instead of conflict.

And once cooperation is present, conversion becomes an act of alignment instead of resistance.

The Three Pillars of Invitational Selling

You now understand the three pillars of Invitational Selling™:

- Build Genuine Rapport

- Communicate Your Unique Value

- Invitation, Not Pressure

In simple terms, these become the rhythm of every effective sales conversation:

Connect. Convey. Convert.

Now that you understand the power of Invitational Selling™, the next step is learning how to apply it in everyday conversations. In the next chapter, we will turn these principles into simple, practical tools you can use immediately. This is where the system becomes repeatable, reliable, and ready to use in any conversation.

Key Takeaways:

- Pressure creates buyers' remorse, invitation creates ownership.

- People say yes more often when they feel free to say no.

- Invitations must be clear, confident, respectful, and open.

- Autonomy increases trust, which increases commitment.

- The goal is not to close, the goal is to open a door.

CHAPTER 7

The Psychology Behind Invitational Selling

Why Trust, Autonomy, and Story Create the Conditions for a Natural "Yes"

Before anyone decides what to buy, they decide whether or not to trust. And that decision happens long before logic, features, or benefits ever enter the picture. Trust, safety, and connection are the real engines behind every yes. They open the mind, lower the guard, and allow people to consider what you are offering without feeling pressured or defensive.

When people feel safe with you, they listen differently, they think differently, they decide differently.

That is the heart of Invitational Selling™.

This chapter is not about scripts or techniques. It is about the psychology beneath all of it, the human wiring that determines whether someone leans in or shuts down. When you understand why people behave the way they do, the entire sales conversation becomes simpler, cleaner, and far more natural.

Let's break down the forces that make Invitational Selling™ so effective.

How Trust and Connection Drive Decision-Making

If you have ever watched someone try to make a decision while they were uncomfortable, you already know the outcome. They freeze, they hesitate, they second-guess. Their brain is no longer evaluating your offer, it is evaluating you.

But when they sense safety, sincerity, and humanity, that system relaxes. Emotion leads, logic follows.

This is why connection comes before conversion. Connection opens the mind so your message can land. When someone feels connected to you, their mind shifts from defensive to open. When they do not, every word you say lands with suspicion.

Trust does not require perfection; it requires presence. Connection does not require charisma; it requires sincerity.

Invitational Selling™ begins with a simple truth:

You cannot guide someone until they trust you enough to follow.

"People decide to trust you long before they decide to buy from you."

Now let's go a level deeper into the specific behaviors that create trust instantly.

TRUST TRIGGERS

The Small Signals That Create Big Confidence

Ditch The Pitch

In sales, people do not buy the pitch; they buy the person delivering it. With the rise of AI-generated content where everything feels polished, automated, and predictable, buyers are craving something simple, human, and real.

Trust is not built through persuasion, pressure, or perfection.

It is built through subtle signals and consistent cues that tell someone:

I like you.

I believe you.

I feel safe moving forward with you.

These micro-moments are what I call Trust Triggers. They are essential to Invitational Selling™ because an invitation only works when it is extended by someone the buyer feels good about.

Here are the core Trust Triggers your prospects are always evaluating whether consciously or not.

---

1. Presence Over Performance

Your presence is your most powerful asset. A person decides if they trust you long before they decide if they will buy from you.

Presence triggers trust. Performance triggers suspicion.

Buyers feel more at ease when you:

- Show up calm, grounded, and attentive

- Allow them to feel seen, not scanned

- Listen without rehearsing your next line

Presence says, "I am here with you."

Performance says, "I am here to get something from you."

Your prospects feel the difference immediately. Presence is how you **connect** and create safety.

2. Consistent Micro-Alignment

Trust collapses when words and actions do not match. It skyrockets when they do.

You create micro-alignment when you:

- Do what you said you would do

- Start and end on time

- Follow up when you promised

- Treat every person with equal respect

- Keep the small commitments, not just the big ones

Each small match between your words and actions whispers, "You can rely on me."

Reliability builds trust faster than charisma ever will. This is how you **convey** integrity without ever needing to announce it.

3. Respecting Autonomy

Autonomy is one of the most powerful psychological needs humans have. When autonomy is supported, confidence increases, motivation rises, and commitment strengthens.

One of the fastest ways to erode trust is to push. One of the fastest ways to build trust is to allow space.

Simple autonomy-supporting statements include:

- "Move forward only if it feels right for you."

- "I want this to serve you, not pressure you."

- "Take a moment, does this fit where you are headed right now?"

Autonomy lowers defenses instantly.

Pressure activates resistance instantly.

"Clarity builds comfort and comfort creates the space where decisions become easy."

When someone feels safe, they become open. When someone feels open, they can think clearly. This is the connection between autonomy and **conversion**.

4. Competence Without Ego

People trust competence, but they connect with humility. Showing expertise without arrogance is one of the strongest credibility signals.

You trigger this when you:

- Speak plainly instead of academically

- Answer questions directly

- Admit when you do not know something

- Share real stories and experiences

Competence builds belief.

Humility builds connection.

Together, they build trust.

---

5. Story Signals

Your Differentiating Story™ is one of the strongest trust triggers you possess.

Stories create cognitive ease, which means the brain finds them easier to absorb than facts or charts. When the brain finds something easy to process, it automatically rates it as more truthful.

Your micro-stories reveal:

- Why you care

- What you have learned

- How you have helped

- What matters to you

Stories signal humanity, and humanity signals safety. This is where **connection** becomes emotional, not just informational.

Lauren's story works not because of the bracelet but because of the heartbeat behind it.

Every seller should have three to five story signals ready to share.

---

6. Transparency Without Over-Explaining

Transparency is a trust accelerant. Over-explaining is a trust killer.

Buyers trust statements like:

- "Here is what this costs and why."

- "Here is what I can promise and what I cannot."

- "Here is what most people ask before they decide."

This reduces cognitive load and makes decisions feel simple, clean, and safe.

Transparency builds certainty.

Clarity builds comfort.

Comfort supports **conversion**.

---

7. The Invitation Itself

A clean, confident invitation communicates one powerful message:

"I trust you to make your own decision."

That is the deepest trust trigger of all because people trust the person who trusts them.

Invitations activate autonomy.

Pitches activate resistance.

Why Autonomy Increases Commitment

When people feel pushed, their instinct is to pull back. When they feel invited, their instinct is to lean in.

Behavioral science shows that when someone chooses freely, three things happen:

- They defend their decision

- They follow through more consistently

- They feel confident instead of conflicted

Pressure produces compliance, and compliance is fragile. Invitation produces commitment, and commitment is durable.

This is why Invitational Selling™ dramatically reduces buyer's remorse. People rarely regret decisions they freely chose.

"Invitation activates autonomy and autonomy turns a decision into a commitment."

Why Stories Beat Stats Every Time

Humans do not think in data; we think in narrative.

Stories:

- Bypass resistance

- Create emotional resonance

- Help people imagine themselves in the experience

- Activate memory and meaning

When the mind enters a story, defensiveness drops and receptiveness increases.

Facts inform.

Stories transform.

Moving From Transaction To Partnership

Traditional sales is adversarial. One person pushes, the other defends.

Invitational Selling™ shifts the dynamic entirely. You stand with the prospect rather than opposite them.

Partnership language sounds like:

- "Let's explore this together"

- "We can look at whether this makes sense.

- "Here is a direction that might help"

- "What would you like your next step to be?"

When the conversation feels collaborative, decisions feel lighter and clearer.

People do not want to be sold. They want to be supported.

Why This Matters More Than Ever

People are skeptical. They have been pitched, pushed, pressured, persuaded, and closed more times than they can count.

Connection cuts through the noise.

Autonomy lowers defenses.

Story breaks down barriers.

Partnership builds trust.

Invitation creates action.

This is not a technique. It is not a hack. It is not a trick.

It is a deeply human way to communicate, one that aligns with how people naturally make decisions.

In the next chapter, we will take this psychological foundation and turn it into a practical, three-part framework you can use in any conversation. It is simple, it is natural, and it makes selling feel good on both sides of the table.

Key Takeaways:

- Invitation honors the way the brain prefers to decide.

- Connection produces serotonin and reduces stress.

- People follow through more when they choose the action themselves.

- Decision quality improves when people feel supported rather than pushed.

- Influence rises when pressure disappears.

CHAPTER 8

Invitational Selling Formula

Connect → Convey → Convert™

Selling becomes dramatically easier when the conversation follows a natural human rhythm, not a script, not a pitch, not a performance. A rhythm. A flow. A human sequence.

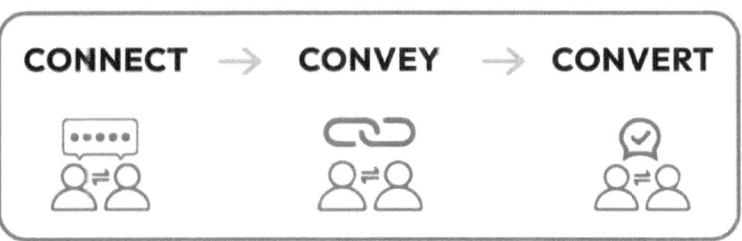

This is the framework of Invitational Selling™. It is simple, it is repeatable, and it works across industries, roles, and every type of meaningful conversation.

Most sales fall apart when the seller jumps ahead. They rush, they skip steps, or they assume understanding before it exists. But when you follow this three-part flow, something powerful happens:

People relax.

People open-up.

People think clearly.

People choose willingly.

"People relax when they feel seen, they engage when they feel understood, they choose when they feel in control."

Before we break down each stage, consider a story that demonstrates what happens when even one part of the flow is missing.

A short while ago, I was working with a senior executive from one of the largest industrial construction services companies in the Southwest. He told me about a lunch he'd recently had with a long-time client he hadn't seen in a while. During the conversation, the client mentioned they were struggling to manage their technology infrastructure and were frustrated with the lack of support from their current provider.

The executive listened, stunned. His company offered exactly those services — fractional CTO support, infrastructure management, cybersecurity — but the client had no idea. The executive realized he had never conveyed those capabilities, nor had he connected deeply enough in the past for the client to feel comfortable sharing those challenges sooner.

By the time they had that lunch, the client had already chosen another provider. "I wish I had known you did that," the client said. "I would have worked with you."

Both men left the conversation frustrated, not with each other, but with the missed opportunity. A lack of connection, and a lack of two-way conveying, led the client to convert in the only direction he believed was available. Someone else.

This is why Connect → Convey → Convert™ matter.

When one piece is missing the entire opportunity disappears.

Let's walk through what each stage looks like in real conversations.

---

1. CONNECT

"I see you."

Connection is the foundation of every meaningful interaction.

It is not small talk, it is not chit-chat, and it is not wasted time. Connection creates psychological safety, and psychological safety determines whether the other person's brain opens up or shuts down.

When someone feels seen, heard, and respected, their brain produces serotonin. Serotonin promotes calm, comfort, and openness, which means they are more willing to share honestly, listen openly, and explore possibilities with you.

When connection is missing, the brain shifts into alert mode. That internal voice whispers, *"Be careful here."* Tension rises, resistance increases, and the conversation becomes guarded.

Your job is simple:

Before you guide, connect.

Before you teach, connect.

Before you explain anything, connect.

Real connection sounds like:

"Good to see you again."

"How are things going on your end?"

"Before we dive in, catch me up on what's been happening."

"I'm glad we get a chance to talk today."

It is not complicated.

It is human.

2. CONVEY

"Let's understand each other."

Once connection is established, you move to Convey — the most misunderstood and most essential stage of Invitational Selling™.

Conveying is not pitching.

Conveying is not presenting.

Conveying is not talking at someone.

Convey means **two-way understanding**. You convey understanding and information to them, and you invite them to convey understanding and information back to you. It is a mutual exchange that clarifies the situation, reveals what matters most, and builds the trust required for a meaningful decision.

"Convey equals two way understanding."

Conveying is not interrogation.

You are not dragging someone through a checklist.

You are not performing an inquisition.

You are not "setting them up" for a sale.

Instead, Convey is rooted in curiosity. It is the belief that the more you understand each other, the more accurate, valuable, and personalized the next step becomes.

Examples of effective conveying questions include:

"What is the biggest challenge you're facing with this?"

"What have you already tried?"

"What matters most to you here?"

"What would an ideal outcome look like?"

"Can I reflect something back to you to make sure I'm understanding correctly?"

You are not trying to extract information.

You are trying to understand a human being.

And when people feel understood, they move toward you.

"Conveying is not pitching, conveying is understanding and being understood."

This is why Convey is the bridge between connection and choice. It builds clarity, strengthens rapport, reduces tension, and creates alignment — everything a person needs before they can confidently decide.

---

3. CONVERT

"Here's your opportunity to choose."

If Connect opens the mind and Convey opens the heart, Convert opens the path.

Convert does not mean closing.

Convert does not mean pushing.

Convert does not mean manipulating the moment.

Convert means offering a simple, clear opportunity for them to make a decision that matters.

Conversion, in Invitational Selling™, is not something you do to someone.

It is something you allow them to do for themselves.

You are not forcing change.

You are allowing them to choose change.

Concrete examples of Convert language include:

"If it makes sense, we can explore what the next step looks like."

"Would you like to see what this could look like moving forward?"

"If you'd like, I can walk you through your options."

"Want to take a look at what working together might involve?"

Nothing pressured.

Nothing clever.

Nothing dramatic.

Just an authentic invitation to consider the next step.

"Conversion becomes effortless when clarity and autonomy lead the way."

When you connect first, convey second, and convert last, resistance disappears and willingness rises. People make decisions easily when they feel safe, understood, and respected.

Autonomy also activates the brain's dopamine pathways — the circuits associated with motivation, ownership, and follow-through. When people feel the decision is theirs, not yours, their brain rewards the choice internally. That internal reward is what makes people commit and stay committed. Pressure shuts this down. Autonomy turns it on.

Common Mistakes That Break the Flow

Even seasoned professionals slip out of the Connect →
Convey → Convert™ rhythm. These are the most common
breakdowns.

- **Skipping Connection**

  When you start too fast, people tighten up. If they
  don't feel seen, they won't open up.

- **Talking Instead Of Conveying**

  Explaining is one-way. Conveying is two-way. If you
  talk too soon, you miss the information you actually
  need.

- **Asking Questions Without Curiosity**

  People can feel the difference. Real curiosity opens
  doors. Scripted questions shut them.

- **Not Reflecting Back What You Heard**

  Reflecting back someone's words affirms that you
  were listening. It shows alignment, not repetition.

- **Rushing The Convert Step**

  Convert is an invitation, not a push. People convert
  when they are ready — your job is to create the
  conditions, not the pressure.

- **Assuming They Know What You Offer**

  Many rejections are simply misunderstandings. If you haven't conveyed it clearly and fully, they can't choose it.

These aren't failures. They're signals. They show you exactly where the flow broke — and exactly where to improve next time.

Why This Flow Works

This sequence works because it aligns with the way the human brain makes decisions.

Connection Lowers Resistance

When someone feels safe, their brain relaxes and listens.

Conveying Builds Clarity And Trust

When someone feels understood, they open up and engage.

Conversion Becomes A Natural Next Step

When someone knows their options and feels no pressure, they choose confidently.

The flow builds momentum because each step prepares the mind for the next.

Skip ahead, and you lose them.

Follow the rhythm, and everything feels natural.

Lauren demonstrated this instinctively on the beach, selling bead bracelets.

She connected first, making people feel welcome.

She conveyed by listening, asking simple questions, and responding to what they said.

And she allowed people to convert, not by pushing, but by giving them the space and autonomy to choose.

What she did intuitively is the very structure you are learning to do intentionally.

That tone, that rhythm, that energy is what you are learning to replicate, authentically, respectfully, and without pressure. And once you understand this flow, the next question becomes clear: what gets in the way of it? What breaks trust? What blocks connection? That is where we go next.

Where We Go Next

Now that you understand that flow of Connect → Convey → Convert™, it is time to explore something equally important:

Why traditional sales tactics damage trust.

Why pressure closes minds instead of opening them.

123

And why collaboration and partnership create results persuasion cannot.

That's where we're headed next.

Key Takeaways:

- Connect → Convey → Convert™ mirrors the natural rhythm of human decision-making.

- Connection lowers resistance, conveying builds trust and clarity, conversion opens possibility.

- Following the flow prevents misunderstandings and reduces tension.

- This framework works in sales, leadership, coaching, hiring, and daily life.

- Human conversations, not scripts, create the strongest results.

CHAPTER 9

From Pitch To Partnership

How Connection Creates Commitment

Most salespeople don't lose business because their product is wrong; they lose it because their approach is wrong.

Traditional sales, what I call "pitch-based selling," is built on one core belief:

If I push hard enough, you'll eventually say yes.

But here's the truth that every buyer, client, and audience member already knows:

Pressure creates resistance; invitation creates partnership.

This chapter is about helping you shift from being someone who "pitches" to someone who "partners," because partnership is what people actually want, and it is what creates action that lasts.

Pressure breaks connection before the conversation even begins. Invitation restores it. And once connection is re-established, clarity becomes possible, which is the foundation of every confident decision.

"Pressure breaks connection, invitation builds it."

Why Traditional Sales Breaks Trust

For decades, sales training taught people to "overcome objections," "handle resistance," and "close hard."

But think about what each of those phrases implies.

The client is resisting you.

You must overcome them.

You must apply more pressure.

They must be "closed," as if they are a problem to solve instead of a person to serve.

None of this creates trust.

None of this creates safety.

None of this feels good.

And here's the real kicker:

Nobody likes feeling trapped, and nobody buys joyfully when they feel cornered.

Pressure activates the part of the brain that says,

"I don't trust this."

"I'm not ready."

"Back off."

Once the brain goes there, the conversation is already lost.

Push Vs. Pull. Close Vs. Invite. Transaction Vs. Partnership.

Let's compare the two worlds clearly.

PUSH (Traditional Selling)

- "Let me tell you why you need this."

- "Let me show you everything we offer."

- "Let me get you to the close."

The salesperson does all the talking.

The buyer feels hunted.

PULL (Invitational Selling™)

- "Tell me what you're trying to accomplish."

- "Let me understand what matters most to you."

- "Would you like to explore a next step?"

The conversation is cooperative.

The buyer feels respected.

One pushes toward an outcome, the other pulls toward clarity.

One is about getting the sale, the other is about helping the person.

One creates resistance, the other creates partnership.

Pull-based, invitational conversations enhance clarity, which is the essence of the Convey stage. When clarity rises, confidence rises. And when confidence rises, conversion becomes a natural, unforced next step.

This shift is not subtle, it is transformational.

"People don't resist clarity, they resist pressure."

How Invitational Selling™ Wins In Any Economy

In tightening economies, people become more cautious, more selective, and more sensitive to pressure.

The more uncertain the world becomes, the more people seek trust, transparency, and truth.

That is why Invitational Selling™ thrives in any market.

It is built on principles the human brain is wired to respond to:

- Autonomy increases commitment

- Agency increases ownership

- Clarity increases confidence

- Safety increases openness

- Respect increases trust

When someone feels that you care about their goals more than your own agenda, they lean in.

When they feel safe, they think clearly.

When they think clearly, they decide confidently.

When they decide confidently, they rarely go backward.

You don't have cancellations.

You don't have buyer's remorse.

You don't have clients disappearing the moment they walk out the door.

The conversion moment creates durable decisions because the choice belongs to the client.

Most sales fall apart not because the Convert stage is weak, but because the Connect and Convey stages were never fully completed. Conversion is not an event; it is an outcome of alignment.

Where Sales Fall Apart (Especially For Speakers)

I see this constantly with the speakers I coach.

They deliver an incredible presentation, they inspire, they teach, they connect.

The audience is with them the entire time.

And then they get to the end … and everything collapses.

Here's what it usually looks like:

1. **They Run Out Of Time**

   Now the conversion moment becomes a frantic blur.

2. **They Rush The Offer**

   They trip over the details, speed up their voice, or skip key information.

3. **They Tighten Up**

   Their natural delivery disappears, their energy shifts, the audience feels the pressure spike.

4. **They Forget The Offer Entirely**

   (Yes, this happens all the time.)

But the root causes are almost always the same:

- Lack of practice

- Lack of awareness about how to transition

- Discomfort around selling

- Fear of judgment

- Fear of looking pushy

- Fear of rejection

- Breakdown in the convert stage

And here's the important part:

None of these fears help your audience.

In fact, avoiding the invitation actually hurts them.

Why?

Because the people in your audience, or on the other end of your sales call, want help.

They want clarity.

They want direction.

When you fail to invite, they walk away with inspiration, but without a path.

Partnership never happens.

Partnership Begins When You Stop Performing And Start Serving

The moment you stop trying to craft the perfect pitch and start trying to help the person in front of you, everything changes.

Your tone changes

Your energy changes

Your confidence changes

Your clarity changes

Your results change

Because people can feel the difference between these two mindsets:

"I need this sale."

vs.

"I want to help you."

The second one creates connection.

The second one creates credibility.

The second one creates commitment.

Partnership is born the moment the client senses one thing:

You care more about their outcome than your performance.

That is the moment Invitational Selling™ becomes real.

"Partnership is the moment the buyer feels you care about their outcome more than your agenda."

From Selling To Serving, From Serving To Solving, Leading Naturally To Partnership

Here's the natural progression:

CONNECT

"I see you."

CONVEY

"I understand you."

CONVERT

"I can help you if you want help."

Which leads to:

PARTNERSHIP

"Let's solve this together."

This Progression reflects the heart of the Connect → Convey → Convert™ model and how it naturally leads to partnership.

Partnership builds something no pitch ever could:

Mutual respect.

Mutual commitment.

Mutual success.

Partnership is the ultimate expression of the Convert stage, not a pressured yes but a mutually chosen path forward.

The Invitational Selling™ Cycle

Partnership isn't the end of the process. It is the beginning of a deeper one.

When you move someone through Connect, Convey, and Convert, you create partnership, and partnership always increases connection.

That new connection leads to more clarity.

More clarity leads to more confident decisions.

More confident decisions strengthen the relationship again.

Invitational Selling™ is not linear, it is cyclical.

Every partnership elevates the next interaction.

This is why great relationships deepen over time.

Each cycle builds trust, reinforces value, and makes future collaboration more natural, more human, and more effortless.

Key Takeaways:

- Pitching pushes, partnership aligns.

- People want to collaborate, not be convinced.

- Coaching someone through their thinking works better than trying to override it.

- When you communicate shoulder-to-shoulder, decisions feel shared, not imposed.

- The best partnerships begin with respect and end with mutual commitment.

CHAPTER 10

Language Of Invitation

Inviting The Next Step, The Conversation That Makes Action Feel Natural

Invitational Selling™ is simple. Once you have built genuine rapport, understood their needs, and clearly communicated your value, there is only one thing left to do.

You invite.

Not pressure,

Not push,

Not "close,"

Just invite.

Most sales fall apart not because the offer is wrong, but because the invitation is unclear, uncomfortable, rushed, or avoided entirely.

I see this all the time with the speakers I coach. They deliver an incredible presentation. They connect deeply.

They tell great stories. The audience is fully engaged. And then, in the last three minutes, everything changes.

Some speakers run out of time and rush through an awkward, last-second pitch.

Some forget to make the offer entirely.

Some tighten up so much their natural delivery disappears.

In my experience, this usually happens because of four things:

- Lack of practice

- Lack of awareness about how to transition confidently

- An unspoken fear of selling

- And the biggest one of all, the fear of rejection

These fears rarely show up as loud emotions. They sneak in quietly. A tightening in the chest, a slight hesitation, a shift in tone. The speaker begins thinking about themselves instead of the audience, and the natural, human rhythm of the conversation collapses. What was warm becomes awkward, what was clear becomes rushed, and what was flowing becomes forced. None of this benefits the audience, and it certainly does not benefit you.

When you avoid or rush the invitation, your audience misses the chance to get the help they were hoping you would offer, and you miss the opportunity to serve them at a deeper level.

Invitational Selling™ fixes all of that.

Here is where the Convert™ Phase of Connect → Convey → Convert™ truly comes to life. Conversion is not an event. It is an experience of clarity where someone feels understood, supported, and safe enough to take the next step. Invitation is the bridge that carries them there.

"Invitation is not persuasion, it is clarity with kindness."

The Purpose of an Invitation

An invitation does one thing:

It gives someone a clear, comfortable path forward.

That's it.

Without an invitation, people feel stuck and unsure. They may even feel confused, and you remember what we said about cognitive dissonance. When someone does not understand what comes next, their mind slips into uncertainty, and uncertainty never leads to a yes. Clarity does, direction does, invitation does.

People do not want pressure. They want direction.

"Invitation is leadership without pressure."

A well-crafted invitation gives them both direction and choice, which is why it sits at the heart of Invitational Selling™.

The Structure of an Invitational Selling™ Conversation

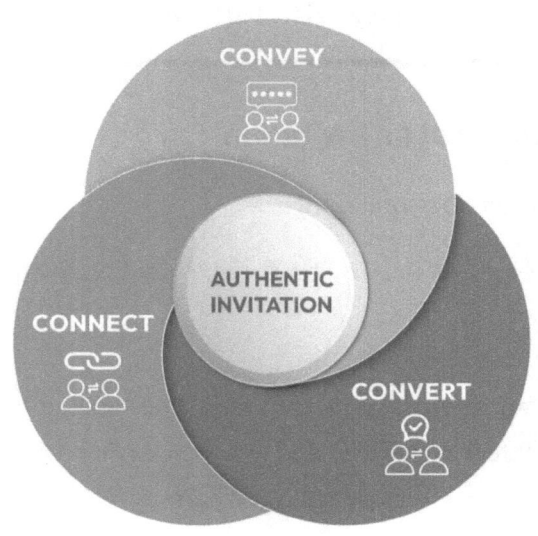

CONNECT — CONVEY — CONVERT

Here is the core flow:

Connect

> **Relationship** - "I see you."

Convey –

> **Understanding** - "I get what you're dealing with."

> **Value** - "Here's how I can help."

Convert

> **Invitation** - "Would you like to take the next step?"

That third step is where most people freeze, but it is actually the easiest.

Invitations are simply questions, questions delivered with kindness, clarity, and options.

Micro-Invitations and Macro-Invitations

There are two types of invitations you will use.

1. Micro-Invitations

Small, easy yeses that create comfort.

Examples:

"Would you like a resource that explains this?"

"Want to see how that works?"

"Would it help if I walked you through an example?"

"Want me to show you the next step?"

Micro-invitations gently move the conversation forward.

2. Macro-Invitations

These invite the person into a meaningful next step.

Examples:

"If you'd like, we can talk about what working together might look like."

"Would you like help implementing this?"

"If it makes sense, we can set up a time to dive deeper."

"I'm not sure if this is right for you, but we have something you might be interested in. Want the details?"

Macro-invitations land best when micro-invitations have already created trust.

Both types are strengthened by one mindset:

You are responsible for the effort, not the outcome.

Why Invitations Work

Invitations work because they:

1. **Lower Pressure**

   They respect the person's freedom to choose.

2. **Create Clarity**

   People cannot say yes if they do not understand what comes next.

3. **Demonstrate Leadership**

   People want guidance when the decision matters.

When you invite with sincerity, people feel cared for, not sold to.

The Power of Options

Providing options increases autonomy and reduces defensiveness.

Examples:

"We can approach this two ways. Which works better for you?"

"Some clients start with A, others start with B. What feels right for you?"

"We can move forward now or set up a time next week. What is better for you?"

Options increase ownership. Ownership increases follow-through. Follow-through reduces buyer's remorse.

"Options create ownership, ownership creates action."

When people choose willingly, they stand behind their decisions. When they feel pressured, they doubt their decision the moment they walk away.

Invitational Selling™ dramatically reduces cancellations, refund requests, and post-purchase regret because your clients feel empowered, not pushed.

A Boardroom Invitation That Changed the Outcome

Several years ago, I was brought into a mid-sized organization to help address declining engagement and inconsistent performance across the leadership team.

The CEO was frustrated.

Turnover was rising.

Execution was uneven.

And trust between departments was strained.

After a day of interviews and observation, the solution was clear to me. They needed focused leadership alignment work, ongoing communication training, and a structured follow-through process.

What would *not* work was telling them what they "had to do."

Instead of presenting a recommendation as a directive, I framed the conversation differently.

I said:

"Based on what I've seen, there are two ways organizations typically move forward at this point."

Then I laid out the options.

Option one was minimal, a short workshop designed to create awareness and shared language.

Option two was more comprehensive, a multi-month engagement focused on alignment, leadership communication, and sustained execution.

Then I paused and asked a simple question:

"Which approach feels like it would serve your team best right now?"

I did not rush to fill the silence.

I did not justify or defend either option.

I let the room breathe.

After a short discussion among the leadership team, the CEO looked back at me and said:

"If we're going to do this, we should do it right. Let's go with option two."

What mattered most was not which option they chose.

What mattered was that *they chose it*.

Because they chose it:

- Buy-in was immediate

- Participation was high

- Resistance was minimal

- Follow-through was consistent

There was no second-guessing later.

No internal sabotage.

No quiet resentment about being "sold" something.

The invitation created ownership, and ownership created results.

That is the power of language that invites rather than instructs.

What to Say When You Are Not Sure What to Say

Here are simple, pressure-free invitations you can use anytime:

"Would you like to explore this further?"

"I'm happy to show you what this could look like."

"If it makes sense, we can look at your options."

"Would it help to take a look together?"

"If you'd like, we can talk about whether this is a fit."

Notice these do not push. They open doors.

The Secret to Making Invitations Feel Natural

Invitations only feel awkward when you are thinking about yourself.

"How do I sound?"

"Am I being too pushy?"

"What if they say no?"

Shift the focus to them.

"Will this help them?"

"Will this make their life easier?"

"Is this something they want to explore?"

"Will this move them closer to the result they want?"

When you care more about their outcome than your performance, invitations feel natural.

Think about Lauren:

She did not overthink her approach.

She did not worry about rejection.

She did not fear looking awkward.

She simply made an honest, human invitation:

"How many would you like?"

Not pressured

Not complicated,

Just caring and confident

Your invitations can feel the same

The Most Natural Invitation in Sales

Here is the sentence I teach almost every client:

"If you'd like help with this, I'd be happy to show you what that could look like."

Soft

Clear

Respectful

Human

That is the essence of Invitational Selling™.

The language of invitation gives people room to choose. Your story gives them a reason to care. When the two work together, your conversations become natural, honest, and deeply compelling. Before you ever invite someone to take a next step, your Differentiating Story creates the trust that makes that invitation feel safe. In the next chapter, we will explore how to shape that story so people feel connected to you long before you ever ask for action.

"Your job is the effort, not the outcome."

Key Takeaways:

- Language shapes emotional tone, and tone shapes decisions.

- Invitational language reduces tension and increases engagement.

- Phrases like "if it makes sense," "when you are ready," and "would you like ..." create safety.

- The right words can shift a conversation from guarded to open in seconds.

- People remember how you made them feel, not how perfectly you delivered your script.

CHAPTER 11

Your Differentiating Story

How Your Story Becomes Your Most Powerful Invitation

Your Differentiating Story™

How your story becomes your most powerful invitation

If you want people to listen, trust, and act, there is one element of communication that cuts through noise faster than anything else.

Story.

Not a pitch.

Not a script.

Not a perfectly worded explanation.

A story.

Stories slip past the pressure, bypass the resistance, and speak directly to the part of the brain that decides whether someone feels connected to you.

Logic informs, story transforms. Data makes you smart, but a story makes you memorable.

And in a world where AI now generates more sales messages than actual humans, your personal story, and the emotion behind it, may be the single most powerful differentiator you have. AI can mimic words, but it cannot duplicate lived experience. It cannot imitate the feeling behind your story. It cannot replicate the humanity that inspires trust.

When AI creates sameness, authentic communication creates distinction, connection, and results.

Your Differentiating Story™ is the part of you no algorithm can replace.

"Your story is the part of you no algorithm can replace."

What a Differentiating Story™ Is (and What It Isn't)

A Differentiating Story™ is the short, true, meaningful moment that reveals who you are behind what you do.

It shows your values. It shows your heart. It shows your journey. And it shows why your work matters to you.

What it is:

- Short

- Emotional

- Relevant

- Authentic

- Purpose-Driven

What it is not:

- Your full autobiography

- A long speech

- A brag

- A performance

- A sales pitch

Your Differentiating Story™ lets people feel you, not just hear you.

Why Your Differentiating Story™ Matters

People do not buy information.

They buy belief

They buy trust

They buy alignment

A strong Differentiating Story™:

- Lowers defenses

- Builds instant rapport

- Creates emotional connection

- Accelerates trust

- Makes your value "click"

- Separates you from anyone else in your industry

- Makes your message unforgettable

- Humanizes you in a way AI will never match

Research shows that people remember stories 22x more than facts alone. Stories activate empathy, mirror neurons, emotional processing, and oxytocin release. They create connection before content, which is why they are the perfect foundation for Invitational Selling™.

Your Differentiating Story™ is the foundation of the Connect phase of Invitational Selling™. It creates safety, trust, and emotional alignment — the conditions people need before they can truly hear your message. Story opens the door. It makes the conversation human. It allows your listener to lean in rather than brace themselves for persuasion.

"Connection before content is what makes your value land with clarity and impact."

The Three Types of Differentiating Stories™

You do not need a dozen stories. One or two is enough.

Your Origin Story

Why you do what you do.

Your "Why This Matters" Story

A defining moment that shaped your values or philosophy.

Your Client Transformation Story

A story that demonstrates the impact of your work.

Once connection is established, your story also strengthens the Convey phase. A clear, authentic story gives context to your value. It helps people understand not just what you do, but why you do it, and why it matters. When people feel connected to you, they interpret your message through a lens of trust rather than skepticism.

Sometimes your best story comes from your children or your upbringing, just like Lauren's story helped shape the entire Invitational Selling™ philosophy.

Real Differentiating Stories™ You Can Model

Every Differentiating Story™ contains three parts: Meaning, Message, and Bridge.

The Meaning is the insight or truth revealed within the story — what the moment taught you. The Message is the lesson that truth communicates to your listener and why it matters to them. The Bridge is the natural transition the story creates for you as the teller, helping you move smoothly into the next phase of the Invitational Selling™ cycle. Meaning gives the story depth, message gives it purpose, and bridge gives it direction.

Using your Differentiating Story™ in this way deepens connection while allowing you to convey your value without listing features, credentials, or services. Instead of putting the listener on the defensive by describing your strengths outright, the story lets them infer the benefit you bring.

This keeps the conversation open, relaxed, and human — and it makes it far easier for the other person to move toward the decision that serves them best.

"Your story lets people infer your value rather than defend themselves against it."

Below are five examples that demonstrate just how versatile the tool can be.

"Your story becomes the bridge that moves the conversation forward without pressure."

1. The Lauren Story (Personal Origin)

Origin Story

When Lauren was little, she could not see the people we approached on the beach. She relied on me to describe who we were walking toward so she could decide how to introduce herself and offer her bracelets. She wasn't nervous or hesitant. She simply shared who she was, what she made, and the love, energy, and intention she put into every bead.

She didn't pitch. She invited.

She didn't pressure. She connected.

And people responded.

That simple lesson from a blind little girl taught me more about communication than any sales training ever did.

Meaning: People respond to sincerity, not performance.

Message: Your story is the part of you people remember.

Bridge: This moment becomes the perfect lead-in to share why your entire approach is built on connection, not performance, and why that matters for anyone you work with.

---

2. The Professional Story (Your Sales Transformation)

Why This Matters Story / Origin Story

When I began speaking, I sold programs from the stage, and I believed in them completely. They changed my life, and I wanted others to experience that same shift. But every time I transitioned into the sales portion, something tightened — my voice, my posture, my energy. I became robotic, and my sales were terrible.

The truth was simple: I was more focused on myself than on serving the audience.

Then I remembered Lauren on the beach.

She wasn't performing. She was sharing.

She wasn't convincing. She was caring.

I shifted from "I need to sell this" to "I want to help them." Within weeks, my results changed. My confidence shifted. And the cancellation rate that plagued other hard-sell presenters practically disappeared for me.

Meaning: People want your help, not your perfection.

Message: Your story shows them *why* your help matters.

Bridge: This story becomes a natural way to shift into sharing how you focus on service rather than performance, and why that approach helps people feel supported instead of sold.

---

3. The Client Story (Kelly Coffey)

Client Transformation Story

Kelly Coffey ran a coaching business helping women improve self-esteem and create healthier success patterns. She cared deeply about her mission but struggled to communicate her value in a way that led to consistent revenue.

After applying the Invitational Selling™ structure and rewriting her webinar with clarity and connection, she re-recorded it within days.

In the next week, her enrollments and income increased by more than 600 percent.

Nothing magical happened. She simply communicated in a way that let people feel her conviction.

Meaning: Your story is often the missing link between struggle and momentum.

Message: People don't buy programs. They buy belief.

Bridge: This moment lets you naturally shift into discussing the kinds of transformations your clients experience when they communicate with clarity and conviction, and the kinds of results they can expect if they choose to work with you.

---

4. The Leadership Story (Organizational Alignment)

Client Transformation Story / Why This Matters Story

I recently worked with a company to unify five separate product lines under one brand. Each division operated in a silo, and most employees didn't understand what the other divisions did. During a single alignment session, we created one clear message that everyone could stand behind.

By the end of the day, they uncovered more than four million dollars in client opportunities that were right in front of them all along.

The real breakthrough wasn't the revenue — it was the connection, clarity, and unity that made that revenue visible for the first time.

Meaning: Clarity creates confidence. Confidence creates alignment. Alignment creates opportunity.

Message: Story is the bridge that helps people see the bigger picture.

Bridge: This story gives you an easy lead-in to explain how your alignment work helps teams communicate more effectively, reduce friction, and identify opportunities they would never spot on their own — and what that could mean for their organization if they choose to partner with you.

---

5. The "When the Buyer Leads" Story (Buyer-Led Action)

Why This Matters Story / Client Transformation Story

In my private consulting work at Pro Speaker Academy, I mentor business owners and professional speakers who use the stage to grow their companies. These clients are already successful, but they come to me because something is holding them back — conversion rates, unclear messaging, or a signature talk that isn't scaling their business.

Before any discussion of working together, I review their videos in detail. Sometimes it's an hour of footage.

Sometimes it's three days' worth. I look at their structure, clarity, story flow, audience engagement, pacing, transitions, and their invitation to action.

When we meet, I walk them through everything I observed. I ask about their goals. I explain what's holding them back and exactly what they can do to improve. I offer value first — before mentioning any kind of engagement.

Then I pause.

Almost every time, the silence creates the space for them to ask the next question:

"Can you tell me more about what you do?"

Then I describe how I work: the preparation, the analysis, and the two full days of one-on-one work where we engineer a promotional talk that elevates their business.

Then I pause again.

And they ask:

"So … how do I work with you?"

When I share the investment — an amount that reflects deep partnership and high-level transformation — they often whistle or say, "Wow, that's significant."

I agree.

And then I explain why the return on investment is even more significant.

Then I offer one final moment of silence.

And they say the words that matter:

"I'd like to work with you."

No pressure.

No persuasion.

No tactics.

They lead.

They choose.

They own the decision.

Meaning: When people feel understood and supported, they move toward the next step on their own.

Message: The most powerful invitation is the one the buyer initiates.

Bridge: This story becomes an easy transition into sharing how your detailed, service-first approach helps clients see exactly what's possible for them — and what working with you can create when they're ready to take the next step.

"The most powerful invitation is the one the buyer initiates."

These moments of connection make the Convert phase feel natural because by the time you extend an invitation, your listener already feels aligned with you.

How to Use Your Differentiating Story™

In the Invitational Selling™ model, your story plays a role in every stage of the process. It helps you **Connect** by building rapport and emotional resonance. It supports **Convey** by giving meaning to your message. And it prepares the way for **Convert**, because when people feel aligned with who you are, moving forward becomes a natural choice rather than a pressured decision.

Share your story:

- Early in the conversation

- When trust needs to be built

- When someone asks *why* you do what you do

- When you want to humanize the interaction

166

- When people seem hesitant

- Right before you extend an invitation

A Differentiating Story™ is not a performance. It is a moment of human connection.

Common Mistakes to Avoid

Avoid:

- Telling a story that is too long

- Oversharing

- Trying too hard to be impressive

- Making yourself the hero

- Repeating the story the same way every time

- Choosing a story unrelated to the listener

Your story should feel *alive, natural, and relevant.*

Where We Go Next

Your Differentiating Story™ is your emotional signature. It is the part of you that AI cannot replicate and competitors can't steal. Your story doesn't replace the invitation; it prepares people to receive it.

Now that you know how to use your story to create trust and connection, it's time to put these tools into everyday conversations that lead naturally to action.

In the next chapter, we will explore how to apply Invitational Selling™ in real-world situations, so your invitations feel natural, comfortable, and easy for people to say yes to.

Key Takeaways

- Your story humanizes you in a way AI can never duplicate.

- People need to know who you are before they can trust what you offer.

- A meaningful story creates an emotional connection instantly.

- Your story is not about being impressive; it is about being real.

- Connection before content is the fastest way to build engagement and trust

CHAPTER 12

Sales Conversations That Feel Good

(And Work Better)

Sales Conversations That Feel Good (and Work Better)

Practical Tools For Invitational Selling, Making It Real, Repeatable, And Ready To Use

Most sales training teaches people what to say.

Invitational Selling teaches people how to be.

Because no matter how good the script is, if the energy behind it feels pushy, forced, or rehearsed, people will feel the pressure even if your words sound polite.

Let me start with something simple and honest:

Most sales scripts sound robotic.

They are stiff.

They are unnatural.

And they suck the life right out of a real conversation.

Invitational Selling is not a script.

It is a philosophy you live.

And now, in this chapter, it becomes a set of practical tools you use every day.

"The right invitation never feels like selling, it feels like helping."

Your Job, Share The Gift, Let Them Choose

Before we get into the tools, I want to share something I deeply believe.

Every one of you reading this book right now has a gift to share with the world. You have a talent, a product, a service, a message, or an experience that can genuinely make someone's life better. Your job is simply to make sure the people who need that gift know it exists.

Your responsibility is the effort.

The decision is always up to them.

You are not responsible for their answer.

You are responsible for showing up with *clarity, sincerity, and confidence.*

Your job is to get as good as possible at explaining:

- What you do

- How it helps

- And how their lives get better when they use it

Then, once the opportunity has been shared, you let them decide the rest.

That is agency.

That is respect.

That is Invitational Selling.

The Three Pillars Become Three Daily Habits

Up until now, we have talked about the three pillars. In practice, they become three daily habits.

Habit 1: Rapport First Every Time

Rapport is not a warm-up; it is the foundation. When people feel psychologically safe, they listen differently.

Examples of rapport-first language:

- "How's your week going so far?"

- "Quick question before we dive in …"

- "I am glad we get a chance to talk."

And here is what not to start with:

- Jumping straight into your pitch

- Diving into features

- Launching into a monologue

Connection always comes before conversation.

Habit 2: State Your Value Simply

Your value statement should be simple, clear, short, and benefit-focused.

Confusing:

"We provide integrated strategic solutions across multiple verticals to empower scalable engagement outcomes."

Clear:

"We help companies communicate their value more clearly so they can grow faster and serve their clients better."

One sounds clever.

The other feels real.

"Confidence is contagious, and your ease becomes their ease."

Habit 3: Make Invitations Part Of Every Conversation

Invitations are small, respectful signals that invite the other person to take the next step without pressure.

Examples:

- "If it makes sense, we can take a look at your options."

- "If you'd like, I can walk you through it."

- "Want to explore how this might help you?"

- "I am not sure if this is right for you, but here is something you might be interested in."

These phrases lower resistance and increase engagement.

The Micro-Skills Toolbox

These small, repeatable skills make every conversation smoother and more effective.

1. The Headline Technique

Lead with the short answer first, then expand.

Without the headline:

"Well, our program has several components, including leadership training, communication development, and value alignment ..."

With the headline:

"We help teams communicate better. Here is how we do that ..."

2. The "Explain It To An 8th Grader" Test

Too complex:

"We integrate cross-functional deliverables to optimize operational bandwidth."

8th-grade version:

"We help your team work better together so everyone gets more done with less stress."

If a thirteen-year-old would get it, so will your clients.

3. The "Don't Make Them Feel Stupid" Filter

Confusing version:

"Our heuristic calibration methodology is designed to …"

Respectful version:

"We use a simple process that helps you get clear on what to do next."

If it risks making them feel dumb, delete it.

4. The Breath And Break Method

Without a break (pressure):

"Okay, so the next step would be to get you signed up, and then we will move into …"

With a break (invitation):

"Let me pause for a moment. Here is the next option if you would like it …"

Your calm becomes their calm.

5. Reflect And Redirect

"I hear that you are feeling overwhelmed with your workload. Here is something that might help …"

Reflection builds rapport.

Redirection builds momentum.

"Invitation turns uncertainty into possibility."

How Invitational Selling Sounds In The Real World

A) Sales conversations

"How many would you like?"

"If it feels right, we can start with the basics."

B) Leadership conversations

"What direction feels right to you?"

"Would you like my support on this?"

C) Customer service

"I can help with that if you'd like to take the next step?"

D) Coaching or mentoring

"I have a thought that might help. Want to hear it?"

E) Everyday life

"This might be helpful. Want it?"

"Here is an idea. Interested?"

Invitational Selling works everywhere because it is not a sales method; it is a human method.

The Four-Step Invitational Communication Model

You can use this model in any conversation.

See them.

Understand them.

Serve them.

Invite them.

This model makes conversations feel natural and cooperative instead of forced and intrusive.

Situational Scripts You Can Use Tomorrow

- "If you feel this could help, the next step is simple."

- "I am here to support you either way."

- "What would you like to do next?"

- "If it makes sense, we can move forward from here."

- "Can I share something that might help?"

- "Want to explore your options together?"

These lines are simple, real, and they work.

Many people read those scripts and feel relief. They finally see how to guide a conversation without pressure. But sometimes seeing examples is not enough. People want to know whether this approach actually works in the real world, especially in situations where confidence feels fragile or where the next step feels intimidating. That is why I want to share the following story. It is a powerful example of what happens when someone shifts from helping without direction to inviting with clarity, confidence, and authenticity.

Case Study: How Invitation Transformed One Woman's Webinar And Unlocked Six Times The Results

Kelly Coffey is the founder of StrongCoffey.com, a coaching company dedicated to helping women build confidence, improve self-esteem, and create healthier patterns of success. Her message is powerful and deeply human, but like many mission-driven professionals, she struggled with one specific challenge. She loved serving her audience, but she did not feel comfortable inviting them to take the next step.

Her webinar was thoughtful and generous. The audience loved the content. They resonated with her story. They trusted her. But while she taught with passion, she felt uneasy transitioning from helping to inviting. Traditional sales approaches felt pushy and did not match her voice. As a result, people left inspired but uncertain about how to continue working with her.

Kelly did not need a new message.

She needed a new way to communicate it.

Together, we redesigned her webinar using the Invitational Selling framework. We clarified the emotional journey her audience was on, strengthened her story flow, and restructured the presentation so her offer felt like a natural next step instead of a sudden shift in tone.

We practiced conversational transitions that made her feel confident inviting action without feeling forced or salesy.

Within a few days, she internalized the structure, re-shot her webinar, and released the new version.

One week later the results were undeniable.

Her conversions multiplied.

Her confidence increased.

Her audience responded enthusiastically.

Kelly summarized the shift this way:

Invitational Selling™

"One week after working with Dennis, I created a new webinar using everything I learned. My sales increased 600 percent. I am making six times more revenue and helping six times more women than before, and having six times more fun. Thank you for taking the fear out of self-promotion and teaching me a system that feels authentic."

Her transformation was not simply financial.

It was emotional.

It was internal.

It was the moment she realized that invitation is not about convincing someone, it is about creating clarity, connection, and choice.

Her audience felt supported.

She felt confident.

And the result was more impact, more clients served, and more growth for her business.

This is Invitational Selling in action.

It changes the way people communicate.

It changes the way they serve.

And it often changes what they believe is possible.

"Helping people think clearly is more powerful than getting them to agree."

The Karma of Invitational Selling

Every person you interact with should leave the conversation better than they entered it.

Even in a sales conversation.

Especially in a sales conversation.

Your goal is not to pitch, your goal is to help.

Sometimes helping means pointing someone in the right direction.

Sometimes it means giving them an insight or tool they can use even if they never buy anything from you.

When people feel respected, helped, and valued, even when they do not buy, they remember you. They remember how you made them feel. And when they are ready, willing, and able, they come back.

That is sales karma.

That is long-term brand building.

That is how reputations are built and trust is earned.

People make confident decisions when they feel seen, understood, and free to choose their own next step. That dynamic becomes even more important in a world where technology shapes so much of how we communicate. In the next chapter, we will explore how to use AI in a way that supports human connection rather than replaces it. Because tools can help you prepare, but only you can create the trust that makes invitation possible.

Key Takeaways:

- Micro-skills create macro-results when they are used consistently.

- Simple phrases can reset tension and open new pathways in a conversation.

- Invitations are not techniques; they are habits of clarity and respect.

- Helping people think clearly is more powerful than trying to get them to agree.

- When conversations feel good, decisions come naturally.

CHAPTER 13

From Cold Call to Warm Welcome

Turning Outreach into Invitation

Cold outreach has a reputation problem, and honestly, it earned it.

Most cold calls feel intrusive.

Most cold emails feel generic.

Most LinkedIn messages feel like they were written by a bot that never learned manners.

And most people avoid doing outreach because they don't want to be "that person."

But here is the truth you already know:

You will never grow your business, influence, or impact if you only talk to people who already know you.

Outreach is not the problem; how outreach is done is the problem.

Invitational Selling™ changes everything.

This chapter will show you how to turn every form of outreach into an invitation, every message into a warm welcome, and every connection into a conversation that actually feels human.

Before we get into the techniques, remember this:

Outreach is simply the Connect stage done with clarity, empathy, and intention.

That small shift ties every message back to the natural rhythm of Connect → Convey → Convert™.

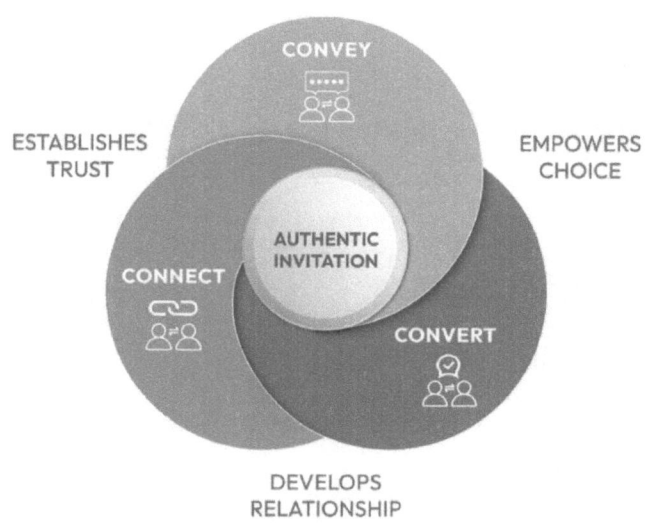

INVITATIONAL SELLING

Why Cold Outreach Fails

Traditional outreach follows three predictable patterns:

1. **It's all about the sender**

   "Can I get 20 minutes of your time?"

   "I want to show you our product."

   "We're doing a big push this quarter."

   Nobody cares.

   People don't respond to neediness; they respond to relevance.

2. **It's designed to trap, not help**

   You know these messages — the pretend question that's really a pitch.

   "How are you scaling your team this quarter?"

   "What strategies are you using to grow revenue?"

   You can feel the setup in your bones.

3. **It demands instead of invites**

   "Book a call."

   "Click here."

   "Schedule this."

Nobody wants to be told what to do by someone they don't know.

People don't resist outreach, they resist pressure.

The Invitational Selling™ Approach to Outreach

Here is the core belief:

Outreach is not about getting attention; outreach is about earning permission.

And the fastest way to earn permission is through:

- Relevance

- Empathy

- Humanity

- Curiosity

- Choice

Let's break this into practices you can use immediately.

---

1. Turn Outreach Into Invitation

A cold message becomes a warm conversation the moment the recipient feels:

- Seen

- Respected

- Not pressured

- Given options

Here is the Invitation Formula for outreach:

A) Start with connection

Not flattery.

Not canned praise.

Real context.

"I saw your post about …"

"I noticed your work in …"

"Someone in my network mentioned …"

Prove you're a human being who actually looked at something they did.

B) Add empathy

Show that you understand their situation.

"Most leaders I work with are dealing with …"

"Many business owners tell me they're overwhelmed by…"

"Lots of associations are struggling with …"

Empathy creates instant relevance.

Value opens the door. Invitation allows them to walk through it.

C) Offer value

Without asking for anything yet.

"I have a short resource that might help if you want it."

"I recently taught a strategy that might be useful."

"I have an idea that could make this easier."

Value earns permission.

D) Invite

Not push.

Not demand.

Invite.

"If you'd like it, I'm happy to share."

"If it makes sense, we can talk briefly."

"No pressure at all; just let me know if this would help."

Your tone makes the difference.

---

2. Lead Generation With Empathy

Empathetic lead generation begins with one question:

"What is their world like right now?"

Great outreach never begins with what you sell; it begins with what they struggle with.

Empathetic entry points include:

"I know the market has been unpredictable …"

"If you're like many leaders I work with …"

"You may be dealing with the same challenge a client of mine just overcame …"

Empathy does two things instantly:

- It shows you understand their reality

- It lowers resistance because empathy never feels like pressure

Empathy opens the door, invitation walks them through it.

3. Networking Without the Cringe

Traditional networking can feel like a room full of people pretending they're not there to sell each other.

Invitational Selling™ fixes this because it removes the performance and replaces it with genuine curiosity.

Here are three simple rules:

Rule 1: Lead with interest, not agenda

Ask about them, their work, their mission, their challenges.

When people feel interesting, they become interested.

Rule 2: Share value without expectation

"I know someone you should meet."

"There's an event you might like."

"Here's a quick idea you can use."

Give without keeping score.

The goal of outreach isn't a meeting. It's a moment of connection.

Rule 3: Invite, don't attach

"If you'd ever like to talk more, I'd enjoy that."

"Happy to connect deeper if it would help."

"No obligation at all; I'm here if you need support."

People are drawn to the energy of someone who isn't trying to get something from them.

---

4. Follow-Up That Feels Like a Service, Not a Nudge

Most follow-up messages feel like guilt trips.

"Just bumping this to the top of your inbox …"

"Did you get my last email?"

"I haven't heard from you yet …"

Awful.

Invitational Selling™ follow-ups feel completely different because the purpose is different:

You're not following up to get something, you're following up to help.

Examples:

"Just sending this in case the timing is better now."

"No pressure at all, but I remembered our conversation and thought this resource might help."

"If this isn't a priority, no worries. I'm here if you ever want support."

Follow-ups like this never annoy people — they're appreciated.

---

5. The Warm Welcome Strategy

Here is the simplest way to transform cold outreach:

Never ask for a commitment before creating comfort.

An outreach message is not an invitation to buy; it is an invitation to engage.

Warm Welcome messages include:

- Relevance

- Empathy

- Humanity

- A small offer

- A pressure-free invitation

This is the formula behind every great first touch.

Invitation creates ownership, ownership creates action.

Now that you can turn cold outreach into warm conversations, it's time to expand the scope.

Invitational Selling™ is not just for sales. The same principles that transform individual conversations can transform entire organizations. When invitation becomes part of your culture, everything changes.

In the next chapter, we'll look at how this philosophy applies everywhere human connection matters.

Key Takeaways:

- Invitational Selling™ works in every outreach scenario because people respond to relevance and empathy.

- Effective outreach uses nuance, not pressure or performance.

- The framework gives you structure while keeping your message authentic.

- When you tailor the invitation to the moment, people feel understood.

- Great communicators adjust their approach without abandoning the method.

CHAPTER 14

Invitation For Every Situation

How Invitational Selling Strengthens Conversations in Work and In Life

Invitational Selling™ is not a sales method; it is a human method.

It works in sales, of course, but it also works in leadership, teaching, coaching, customer service, and even at home with your family.

Once you understand the psychology behind how people make decisions, avoid pressure, and move toward clarity, you realize something important.

Every conversation becomes easier when it feels like an invitation instead of a demand.

Let's explore how this applies across the most important areas of your professional and personal life.

Connection scales what pressure never can.

---

1. Leadership, Inspiring Rather Than Instructing

People do not respond well to pressure, even in the workplace. They may comply, but they will not engage. They may follow orders, but they will not follow you.

Great leaders do not push; they invite.

They set direction, then ask questions like:

"What direction feels right to you?"

"What's your take on this?"

"What options do you think we should consider?"

"What support would help you move forward?"

These questions give the other person ownership, and ownership creates commitment.

Leaders often think their job is to have the answers, but the most influential leaders are the ones who create space for other people's answers to emerge.

Invitational leadership sounds like:

"I trust your judgment, want to talk through your ideas?"

"Would you like my input, or would you prefer to run with it?"

This is not soft leadership; this is smart leadership. It builds cultures where people feel respected, valued, and willing to take action.

Great leaders don't force compliance; they invite contribution.

---

2. Teaching and Coaching, Creating Openness to Learning

Learning requires vulnerability, and vulnerability only happens when a person feels safe.

That is why great coaches and teachers use invitation instinctively:

"Want to try a different approach?"

"Would you like some feedback on that?"

"Want an example that might make this easier?"

Notice the pattern. It is not about authority; it is about collaboration.

Most people shut down the moment they feel judged, but they open up when they feel invited.

As a coach, consultant, or instructor, you are not trying to dominate the room; you are trying to create an environment where insights land, ideas stick, and progress feels possible.

Invitational teaching turns learning into a partnership, not a performance.

The best influence never removes choice; it elevates it.

---

3. Customer Service, Building Loyalty One Interaction at a Time

Customer service is where trust is built or lost, often within seconds.

People reach out because something is wrong, something is unclear, or something is not working. If your answer feels scripted, rushed, or dismissive, the relationship erodes instantly.

But when your customer service team uses Invitational Selling™, the entire experience shifts.

Instead of,

"You need to fill out this form."

"You need to go to this link."

"You need to contact this department."

They say,

"If you would like, I can walk you through the next step."

"We have a couple of options, which one works best for you?"

"I am here to help. Want me to take care of this part for you?"

Suddenly, the customer feels cared for. They feel respected. They feel supported.

This is how loyalty is built, not through perfect products, but through human moments handled well.

4. Personal Life, Influence Without Manipulation

Invitational Selling™ does not just improve business relationships; it improves human ones.

Whether you are talking to your spouse, your kids, or your friends, the same psychology applies.

People do not want to be controlled; people want to be considered.

When your partner feels heard, they open up. When your kids feel respected, they listen. When your friends feel understood, they trust you.

Here are everyday invitations that transform relationships:

"Want to talk about it?"

"Would you like my thoughts, or do you just want me to listen?"

"Do you want help with that, or should I give you space?"

"Would now be a good time, or would later be better?"

This is not manipulation; this is maturity, and maturity strengthens connection.

Pressure closes hearts, invitation opens conversations.

Why Invitational Principles Work Everywhere

Human beings have universal needs:

Autonomy

Respect

Clarity

Safety

Understanding

The desire to choose instead of being told

Invitational Selling™ honors all of these.

It works as well in a boardroom as it does at a dinner table because it reflects how people naturally decide, behave, and bond.

Once you communicate this way consistently, you no longer need to convince people. They walk toward the next step willingly.

Now that you have seen how Invitational Selling™ extends far beyond sales, it is time to address the world we are all navigating.

A world filled with automation, artificial intelligence, digital noise, and endless sameness.

The future of communication will be shaped by technology, but guided by humanity.

The most powerful AI in sales will always be an Authentic Invitation.

Technology may help you communicate faster, but only trust helps you communicate deeper, and trust is what determines whether people embrace your message or move away from it.

Now that you understand how to use AI in a way that strengthens human connection, it is time to bring these skills into real-world situations. In the next chapter, we will explore how Invitational Selling™ shows up in everyday conversations, from first meetings to follow-ups, so your invitations feel natural, clear, and easy to say yes to.

Key Takeaways:

- AI can enhance preparation, but cannot replace human empathy.

- The real competitive advantage is connection, not automation.

- Use AI for information, use your humanity for invitation.

- Technology should amplify your voice, not replace it.

- In a world of sameness, your humanity is your strongest differentiator.

CHAPTER 15

The Invitational Leader

Letting them have your way with you

Leadership has never been about getting people to do what you say.

It has always been about getting people to *believe in what you're building.*

There's an important distinction there, and it's one many leaders miss.

You *can* make people do almost anything as long as you're standing in front of them and carrying a big stick.

You can enforce policies, you can issue directives, and you can monitor behavior.

But the moment you're not in the room, people will do what *they* want to do.

That's not a flaw in your team, it's human nature.

The most effective leaders don't rely on authority alone.

They create alignment.

They don't demand compliance.

They invite commitment.

CONTROL CREATES COMPLIANCE

INVITATION CREATES OWNERSHIP

If your leadership strategy depends on constant oversight, constant correction, and constant reinforcement, you're not leading a team; you're managing behavior.

Behavior management has a short shelf life.

People comply when they feel watched, they disengage when they feel controlled, but they contribute when they feel connected.

The Invitational Leader™ understands something fundamental.

People will protect, defend, and advance what they believe is *their* idea.

THE DIFFERENCE BETWEEN DIRECTION AND DEPENDENCE

Traditional leadership often assumes that clarity requires control.

In reality, *excessive control creates dependence.*

When any decision must be approved, progress slows.

When any idea must be validated, creativity fades.

When any mistake is punished, initiative vanishes.

Invitational leadership works differently.

The leader provides direction without dictating every step.

They offer clarity without micromanagement.

They create a shared understanding of *where* the organization is going and *why* it matters.

Once that foundation is in place, people don't need to be managed; they begin to manage themselves.

"BUY-IN" IS NOT AGREEMENT, IT'S ALIGNMENT"

Buy-in does not mean unanimous agreement on every detail.

It means shared belief in the *direction.*

When people understand the mission, the vision, and the purpose behind the work, they stop asking, "What do you want me to do?" and start asking, "How can I help move this forward?"

That alignment creates momentum, and that momentum creates results.

"I'M GOING TO LET YOU HAVE YOUR WAY WITH ME"

This phrase can feel counterintuitive, especially for leaders who equate strength with certainty and control.

But invitational leadership™ is not about surrendering leadership; it's about surrendering ego

At its core, **"I'm going to let you have your way with me"** is not an abdication of authority, nor is it about the leader being convinced to abandon their own thinking.

It is about something far more strategic.

It is about **presenting an idea in a way that allows others to believe it is theirs**.

When a leader uses this approach, they are not giving up the vision.

They are giving their people the opportunity to *own* it.

What this mindset communicates is:

I will create space for you to arrive at this idea

I will invite your input without needing credit

I will let ownership matter more than attribution

That distinction is critical because people do not commit deeply to ideas they feel were imposed on them. They commit to ideas they believe they helped shape, refine, or discover.

When leaders allow others to take ownership of the idea, even when the original vision came from the leader, something powerful happens.

Resistance drops, defensiveness fades, and commitment and creativity increase.

That level of openness doesn't weaken leadership;

it amplifies it.

When they believe the idea is *theirs*, they act with a level of care, energy, and accountability no directive could ever produce.

The Invitational Leaders™ don't force belief; they create conditions where belief emerge naturally.

"Letting the other person feel that the idea is his or hers not only works in business and politics, it works in family life as well."
— Dale Carnegie

AUTONOMY CREATES POSSIBILITY

One of the most powerful outcomes of invitational leadership is what happens *beyond expectation*.

Command-and-control leadership produces predictable results. You get exactly what you ask for, no more and often less.

Invitational leadership creates space for possibility.

When people are trusted with autonomy, they stop asking "What am I allowed to do?" and start asking "What's possible here?"

That question unlocks creativity.

When you let others take the wheel, They often drive you further than you planned.

AUTONOMY IS NOT THE ABSENCE OF LEADERSHIP IT IS THE EVOLUTION OF IT

Invitational leader™ do not remove structure: the remove unnecessary constraints.

They still define:

- The direction

- The values

- The outcomes that matter (KPIs)

What changes is how people are invited to contribute.

With autonomy comes permission to think, adapt, and act in ways that could never be scripted in advance, and often, that's when unexpected great things happen.

You can manage behavior, or you can inspire belief. Only one of those works when you're not in the room.

WHEN PEOPLE FEEL TRUSTED, THEY THINK DIFFERENTLY

Trust changes behavior.

When people feel trusted, they bring:

- Ideas you didn't ask for

- Solutions you didn't see

- Initiative you couldn't have planned

They operate beyond their anticipated scope, not because they were instructed to, but because they were empowered to.

This is how innovation actually occurs, quietly, organically, and often unexpectedly.

INVITATIONAL LEADERSHIP UNDER PRESSURE

During times of change or uncertainty, many leaders tighten control.

Invitational leaders do the opposite.

They increase clarity.

People don't resist change itself; they resist being excluded from it.

When leaders invite participation, explain the "why," and allow space for contribution, fear diminishes and engagement increases.

Alignment becomes the stabilizing force.

THE LEADER AS CURATOR, NOT CONTROLLER

Invitational leaders don't control every move, but they do curate the environment.

They shape:

- The conversations

- The questions

- The boundaries

By doing so, they leverage collective intelligence instead of relying solely on their own.

Control limits intelligence to one mind. Invitation expands it across the organization.

LEADERSHIP THAT LASTS

Command leadership often ends the moment the leader leaves the room or the organization. Its influence is tied to presence, authority, and enforcement. Invitational leadership is different. It continues long after the leader steps away because it lives in the culture, not the position.

The greatest leaders don't measure success by how many people follow them. They measure it by how many future leaders they help create. When people are invited into belief rather than forced into behavior, leadership becomes transferable. Decisions are made with shared values in mind, not fear of consequences.

Over time, culture becomes the true legacy of leadership. And that culture is not built through enforcement or constant correction. It is built through belief, belief in the mission, belief in the vision, and belief that what we are building together truly matters.

You can manage behavior, or you can inspire belief.
Only one of those works when you're not in the room.

FIVE KEY TAKEAWAYS

- **Compliance is temporary, alignment is durable**
  Invitational leadership creates commitment that lasts beyond your presence.

- **Buy-in comes from involvement, not instruction**
  People support what they help shape.

- **Autonomy unlocks creativity and initiative**
  When people are trusted, they often exceed expectations.

- **Clarity replaces control as organizations scale**
  Culture becomes the mechanism that guides behavior.

- **Invitational leadership creates a legacy, not dependence**

It builds organizations that thrive without constant oversight.

CHAPTER 16

Incorporating AI

Without Losing The Human Touch

Artificial intelligence is everywhere now. It writes emails, drafts proposals, creates videos, analyzes data, and even pretends to be human in chat windows. And while AI can absolutely support your sales process, streamline your workflow, and help you communicate more efficiently, there is one truth we must anchor.

This chapter is not about artificial intelligence as a technology; it is about how to lead, communicate, and invite in a world where AI is everywhere. The goal is not to become more robotic; it is to become more unmistakably human.

AI can assist your invitation, but it can never be your invitation.

Because invitation is human.

Connection is human.

Trust is human.

And influence, real influence, still happens between people, not processors.

Let's look at how to use AI to make your life easier without letting it replace the very thing that makes your sales approach so effective, your humanity.

---

1. Use AI to Support Your Preparation, Not Replace Your Presence

AI is brilliant at gathering information quickly. It can summarize client bios, analyze public data, and help you see patterns that would take hours to uncover manually.

Let AI handle:

- Research

- Drafting Rough Outlines

- Summarizing Long Documents

- Creating First Pass Emails

- Organizing Thoughts Or Lists

But then, and this is where Invitational Selling™ stays human, you bring the meaning.

You add the sincerity, you choose the tone, you decide what matters.

AI can prepare you, but you are the one who connects.

"AI can help you prepare, your humanity is what creates connection."

---

2. Keep Your Voice, Even When AI Writes the First Draft

AI generated messaging tends to sound polished, but not personal. Clear, but not connected. Competent, but not compelling.

Why?

Because it misses one critical ingredient, you.

Your stories, your humor, your quirks, your energy, your emotion, the things that make you you. do not come preloaded into any AI model.

So when using AI to draft:

- Add Your Personality

- Add Your Voice

- Add Your Heart

The draft gets you started. Your humanity finishes it.

---

3. Let AI Increase Efficiency, Not Emotion

AI can automate:

- Follow-up Reminders

- CRM updates

- Meeting summaries

- Lead prioritization

- Email sorting

All of which gives you more time to do what no machine can do.

Be present with the person right in front of you.

Efficiency is AI's job, empathy is yours.

"When AI increases your efficiency, your presence becomes even more valuable."

---

4. Why Human Invitation Still Wins

Let's be honest. AI can beat us at chess. It can beat us at math. It can even beat some of us at spellink. (See what I did there?)

But it cannot beat a genuine human invitation.

And here is why:

A. Humans Read Emotion, Not Just Language.

AI can write sentences, it cannot feel sincerity.

B. Humans Respond To Energy.

AI cannot smile, laugh, or make someone feel safe in a moment of uncertainty.

C. Humans Build Trust Through Micro Signals.

A pause, a breath, a softening of the eyes. None of that is programmable.

D. Humans Create Connection Through Shared Experience.

AI can describe experiences, it cannot share one with you.

E. Humans Can Be Funny, Even If The Jokes Are Terrible.

And let's face it, after writing this entire book, I've probably proven that half my humor comes from pure dad joke energy and the rest from sheer optimism.

But at least it is human.

AI can produce a joke, only a person can deliver one in a way that makes another person feel something. Humor does not land because of the words, it lands because of the relationship.

"Technology can open doors, only invitation can make someone want to walk through them."

---

5. The Moment I Became Lauren's AI

Remember that Fourth of July on the beach with Lauren and Chris. She could not see who we were walking toward, so she relied on me to describe what was ahead, the families, the sunbathers, the couples, the kids. I gave her the information she needed so she could decide how to approach them.

In that moment, I was essentially acting as her AI, feeding her the kind of helpful context that made her invitations easier and more natural.

But I did not make the invitation for her.

Once she understood who was in front of us, Lauren stepped forward with her own confident, human connection.

"Hi, my name is Lauren, how many would you like?"

I only provided the data, she provided the heart.

AI can support the preparation, but it cannot replace authenticity. It can help you understand people, but it cannot connect with them. It can suggest wording, but it cannot care.

Lauren had all the "intel" she needed, but the real influence came from her presence, her sincerity, and the emotional clarity in her invitation.

Even with all the tools in the world, artificial or human, the power is still in the invitation you deliver with your own voice.

---

6. Use AI to Amplify Your Humanity, Not Replace It

AI is not the enemy of human connection, it is an amplifier for it when used correctly.

Here is what AI can do extremely well:

- Help you stay organized

- Help you communicate more consistently

- Help you draft language you can refine

- Help you understand what your audience cares about

- Help you save time on tasks that pull you away from people

And here is what you must bring:

- Warmth

- Empathy

- Clarity

- Invitation

- Presence

When you blend AI's intelligence with your humanity, you get the best of both worlds, clarity without coldness, efficiency without distance, preparation without pressure.

That is the sweet spot of Invitational Selling™ in the modern age.

"The more automated the world becomes, the more your authenticity becomes a competitive advantage."

7. The Future of Sales Is Not Artificial, It's Amplified

AI will not replace sales professionals.

It will replace sales professionals who act like robots.

The ones who thrive will be the ones who:

- Stay human

- Stay curious

- Stay connected

- Stay invitational

Because in a world where AI makes everything faster, louder, and more automated, your humanity becomes your greatest competitive advantage. It always has been, and it always will be.

AI may enhance your efficiency and expand your reach, but the invitation itself is still human, and always will be.

Key Takeaways:

- Pressure breaks trust, invitation builds commitment.

- People follow through when they feel ownership of their decisions.

- Selling, teaching, mentoring, and leadership all work better when people feel respected and emotionally safe.

- Internal alignment creates the external experience your clients feel.

- Invitation is not just a sales technique, it is a communication philosophy that can transform teams and organizations.

CHAPTER 17

The Invitational Organization™

How Invitation Becomes Culture

Most people think of selling as a moment, a script, a meeting, a pitch. But an invitation is far bigger than the words we speak in a sales conversation; it is a way of leading, communicating, and shaping culture.

The most successful organizations do not treat invitation as a tactic; they treat it as a philosophy that influences how people behave, how teams collaborate, and how clients are served.

An Invitational Organization™ is one where every interaction communicates something simple and powerful.

You belong here.

You are safe here.

You have a choice here.

Before we explore the structure of an Invitational Organization™, let me share a real-world example.

It is one of the clearest demonstrations I have seen of what can happen when an entire company moves from pressure to clarity, from silos to connection, and from confusion to shared mission.

A REAL WORLD EXAMPLE: HOW ONE ORGANIZATION BECAME TRULY INVITATIONAL

Companies in construction and heavy industry operate in some of the most demanding conditions in the country. They face workforce safety concerns, benefits administration challenges, insurance complexity, cybersecurity threats, regulatory changes, and nonstop pressure from the jobsite.

One of my clients, a national business services provider supporting these industries, understood this world completely. But internally, they were facing a transformation of their own.

The organization consisted of five distinct product lines that operated like independent companies. Each division delivered real value, yet they functioned in isolation. Employees could describe their own division accurately, but many had only a partial understanding of the others. Some did not know certain divisions existed at all.

This created inconsistency in communication.

It limited collaboration.

It reduced cross-functional awareness.

It made it impossible for the organization to speak with a unified voice.

The executive team recognized that the issue could not be solved by new branding alone. For the upcoming rebrand to succeed, their people needed understanding, connection, and alignment.

That is when I was brought in to guide them through a communication alignment effort centered on clarity and invitation.

We began with a company-wide survey to measure what employees understood about the organization, the divisions, and the value they delivered. We followed with executive interviews to capture leadership's vision for the rebrand and the message they wanted every employee to communicate.

The turning point came during a two-day, company-wide experience.

Every employee participated.

Client-facing teams, administrative professionals, technical specialists, and leadership all engaged in practical, easy-to-understand exercises that clarified the brand, strengthened communication, and showed how all five divisions supported one another.

What happened next was powerful.

Communication became clearer.

Confidence increased.

People listened to each other differently.

Departments that had rarely interacted began collaborating naturally.

Employees understood the company's value with new clarity.

And then something remarkable happened.

Once the team understood the unified brand and learned how to listen for client needs from the perspective of all five divisions, they began identifying opportunities the organization had been missing for years. These were not invented or manufactured; they were real client needs that had previously gone unnoticed because employees were working in silos.

With newfound clarity and connection, the team uncovered more than $4.1 million in previously unrecognized revenue opportunities simply by understanding the brand, listening differently, and serving clients more effectively.

Their Senior Director of Operations summarized it this way:

"Even more impactful was seeing how empowered our people became once they understood not just what to say, but what to listen for when engaging with clients. It elevated confidence across the organization and strengthened how our five product lines work together."

The financial discovery was significant, but it was not the true transformation.

The true transformation was cultural.

The organization became one brand with one voice.

A unified team grounded in clarity, communication, and connection.
An organization that understood how to make every internal and external interaction feel like an invitation.

This is the essence of an Invitational Organization™.

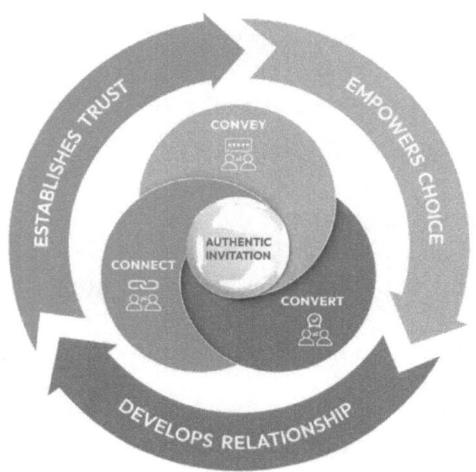

INVITATION ENGINE

"Leaders set the tone, invitation sets the trust."

CULTURE: CONNECTION AS THE OPERATING SYSTEM

Culture is not a slogan, a poster, or a mission statement. Culture is the behavior people choose when no one is watching. In an Invitational Organization™, people choose curiosity over judgment, collaboration over isolation, and clarity over assumption.

Teams become more adaptive.

Communication becomes easier.

People contribute more freely because they feel safe to do so.

Invitation strengthens culture by creating trust, and trust strengthens performance.

LEADERSHIP MESSAGING: INFLUENCE WITHOUT INTIMIDATION

Leaders define how invitation shows up in an organization. Invitational leadership is not permissive; it is clear, confident, and human. Leaders communicate expectations while allowing people to have a voice in how they meet those expectations.

They ask questions.

They invite insight.

They explain the "why" so people understand the direction.

People follow leaders they trust. Invitation builds that trust consistently.

"An Invitational Organization isn't something you say, it's something people feel."

COMMUNICATION: EVERY INTERACTION IS AN INVITATION

Communication is where culture becomes visible.

In an Invitational Organization™, messages are clear, simple, and human. People listen before responding. They seek understanding before influence. They ask clarifying questions instead of assuming resistance.

Communication becomes a bridge instead of a barrier.

ONBOARDING: SETTING THE STANDARD FROM DAY ONE

The first experiences new employees have shape how they interpret everything that follows. Invitational onboarding emphasizes relationship, clarity, and confidence.

New employees should feel welcomed before they feel evaluated.

This creates psychological safety and accelerates integration into the culture.

CUSTOMER EXPERIENCE: THE INVITATION EXTENDS OUTWARD

Customers feel pressure immediately. They feel invitation just as quickly.

In an Invitational Organization™, the client experience reflects the culture behind it.

Customers feel seen.

Customers feel heard.

Customers feel supported.

The organization becomes easier to work with, easier to trust, and easier to recommend.

"When invitation becomes culture, alignment becomes effortless."

THE INVITATIONAL ORGANIZATION™ ASSESSMENT

Use this assessment to evaluate how invitational your organization is today. Check each statement that is currently true for your team.

Culture

- People approach conversations with curiosity

- Connection is encouraged

- Teams collaborate without defensiveness

- Feedback is respectful

- Employees feel psychologically safe

- Wins and effort are acknowledged

Leadership Messaging

- Leaders communicate expectations clearly

- Vision is shared in an inviting way

- Leaders ask questions more than they issue commands

- Decisions are explained with transparency

- Team members feel trusted

- Leaders model what they expect

Communication

- Messages are clear

- People observe before offering advice

- Listening comes first

- Clarifying questions replace assumptions

- Understanding is prioritized

- Internal communication is consistent and human

Onboarding

- New hires feel welcomed

- Relationships begin early

- Expectations are clearly explained

- New employees are encouraged to bring ideas

- Early wins are recognized

- Onboarding communicates trust

Customer Experience

- Customers feel valued

- Problems are approached with empathy

- Options are presented clearly

- Processes feel personalized when appropriate

- Clients receive clear next steps

- The experience communicates belonging

How to Interpret Your Results

- **20–30 checked boxes:** Strong invitational culture with consistent alignment

- **10–19 checked boxes:** Healthy progress with room to strengthen clarity, communication, and connection

- **Below 10 checked boxes:** Invitation is not yet embedded, significant growth potential exists with focused implementation

---

IMPLEMENTING INVITATIONAL SELLING™ ACROSS YOUR ORGANIZATION IN 30 DAYS

Culture shifts quickly when people act with intention. Connect, Convey, Convert™ becomes the rhythm of the entire team, not just individual conversations.

Week One: Build Rapport Across the Company

- Leaders choose one invitational behavior to model daily

- Teams incorporate rapport-building practices

- Everyone practices observing before offering solutions

Week Two: Communicate Unique Value

- Teams clarify who the organization is, what it believes, and how it helps clients

- Internal messages are simplified

- Leaders and staff share Differentiating Stories™ that reinforce the mission

Week Three: Create Clear Invitations

- Teams practice invitational language such as "Are you open to" and "If it makes sense, the next step is"

- Client-facing teams offer options and clarity, not pressure

- Internal conversations shift from direction to collaboration

Week Four: Reinforce and Refine

- Departments select two areas to strengthen

- Teams review the customer journey and identify where invitations can replace instructions

- Leaders gather feedback and celebrate wins

KEY TAKEAWAYS:

- An Invitational Organization™ does not happen by accident.

- It is intentional, it is repeatable, and it is available to any team willing to communicate with clarity, consistency, and respect.

- The principles that guide Invitational Selling™ also guide organizational culture.

- When applied across departments and reinforced by leaders, they create alignment, confidence, and shared purpose.

- Invitation becomes your competitive advantage, not because it pressures people, but because it helps them feel understood.

CHAPTER 18

Conclusion

The Real Win – Seeing Beyond The Sale

If you have made it this far, one thing should be absolutely clear, connection converts, invitation creates commitment.

People may take action under pressure, but they rarely stay committed to those decisions. They do not want to feel pushed, cornered, or talked into something; they want to feel understood and respected. They want to feel like they are choosing, not reacting.

That is why Invitational Selling™ works so well, not only in sales, but in every meaningful human interaction.

It aligns with how people naturally make decisions when they feel safe, seen, and supported. It removes fear and pressure and replaces them with clarity, confidence, and genuine connection.

Traditional sales tactics often fall apart because they rely on force instead of understanding. They create tension instead of trust. They trigger defensiveness instead of curiosity.

Invitational Selling™ does the opposite.

It is effective because it is human.

It is sustainable because it is honest.

It is repeatable because it is simple.

At its core, this entire approach comes down to three things,

Be clear, be sincere, be invitational.

You do not need the perfect pitch.

You do not need a complicated script.

You do not need pressure tactics.

You do not need to be someone else.

What you do need is the confidence to show up authentically, the clarity to express your value simply, and the courage to extend an invitation without being attached to the outcome.

When you do that, something powerful happens:

People trust you.

People return to you.

People recommend you.

People remember how you made them feel.

That is the real win.

THE FINAL THOUGHT I WANT TO LEAVE YOU WITH

As we close this book, I want to leave you with something personal, something meaningful, and something I believe is vital for every opportunity you will ever face.

There is not a day that goes by that I do not think about my daughter, Lauren. She passed away on April 8th, 2015, shortly after her 17th birthday. And while I miss her more than words can express, her memory and her lesson live inside everything I teach.

People often ask how a blind little girl selling bead bracelets on a beach could shape an entire philosophy on communication and sales. The answer is simple. *Lauren did not just teach me how to sell. She taught me how to see.*

She did not have sight,

but she had clarity

She did not have vision,

but she had understanding.

She did not have perfect words,

but she had perfect intention.

And people felt it.

Connection was her instinct,

invitation was her nature.

Her approach was never about pressure. It was never about performance. It was always about sincerity, about helping someone feel seen, safe, and valued.

And that brings me to something I want you to remember as you step forward into the conversations, opportunities, and possibilities ahead.

In life, you are going to be faced with countless chances, chances to serve, to succeed, to grow, to lead, to connect, and to make an impact on the people around you. But with every one of those chances comes a familiar list of questions.

What if I am not smart enough?

What if I do not have the right contacts?

What if I do not have enough money?

What if I do not have the right look?

What if I do not have the right resources?

What if I do not have the right degree?

What if they say no?

And a thousand other "what ifs" designed to slow you down, make you hesitate, or convince you that you are not ready.

But even though every opportunity comes with dozens, if not hundreds, of questions, there is only one question you ever really need to ask yourself.

It is not about whether you have the right degree.

It is not about whether you have the right background.

It is not about whether you are smart enough, experienced enough, or connected enough.

The real question, the one that cuts through fear, doubt, and hesitation, is the question Lauren asked with clarity, sincerity, and possibility on a hot beach on the Fourth of July.

It is a question that invites rather than forces.

A question that reminds us that opportunities are not about worthiness but about willingness.

How many would you like?

CHAPTER 19

APPENDIX

Invitational Language Library™

This Invitational Language Library™ is a complete collection of the words, phrases, and conversational patterns used throughout the book. These examples reflect the core principles of Invitational Selling™, clarity, autonomy, respect, and genuine connection.

Each section begins with a simple explanation written in natural language, followed by real examples you can use in conversations right away.

SECTION 1: Rapport Starters and Connection Openers

These openers help people relax and feel seen. They sound like the beginning of a real conversation, not the start of a sales pitch. Use them to create ease and genuine connection before anything else happens.

- "How's your week going so far?"

- "I'm glad we get a chance to talk."

- "Quick question before we dive in …"

- "Before we get into details, how are things going on your end?"

- "What's been the highlight of your week so far?"

- "Anything important I should know before we begin?"

SECTION 2: Clarifying Questions That Show You're Listening

These questions let people feel understood. They show curiosity without making anyone feel interrogated. Use them any time you want someone to feel genuinely heard.

- "Can you tell me a little more about that?"

- "What result matters most to you right now?"

- "What would make this easier for you?"

- "What's the biggest challenge you're dealing with?"

- "What does success look like for you in this situation?"

- "Would it help if we slowed down and clarified this together?"

SECTION 3: Micro-Invitations

These are gentle prompts that move the conversation forward one small, comfortable step at a time. They lower the pressure and make everything feel easy.

- "Would you like a resource that explains this?"

- "Want to see how that works?"

- "Would it help if I walked you through an example?"

- "Want me to show you the next step?"

- "Would you like to explore that idea a little more?"

- "Would it help if we clarified your options?"

SECTION 4: Macro-Invitations

These invitations offer a meaningful next step without pushing for a decision. They create direction while still giving full control to the other person.

- "If you'd like, we can talk about what working together might look like."

- "Would you like help implementing this?"

- "If it makes sense, we can set up a time to dive deeper."

- "I'm not sure if this is right for you, but we have something you might be interested in. Want the details?"

- "If it feels right, we can look at what the next phase would involve."

- "Would it help to talk through the possibilities?"

SECTION 5: Autonomy-Based Options Language

Options lower stress and raise confidence. When people choose, they commit. These phrases make that choice feel comfortable.

- "We can approach this in two ways. Which works better for you?"

- "Some clients start with A, others start with B. What feels right for you?"

- "We can move forward now or next week. What's better for you?"

- "Would you prefer the deep-dive version or the short overview?"

- "We can do this together, or I can give you a tool to do it yourself. What's best for you?"

- "If you'd like choices, I can lay out a couple. Want that?"

SECTION 6: Value Clarifiers and Benefit Bridges

These phrases connect what you offer to why it actually matters. They help people understand the benefit clearly and quickly.

- "Here's how this can help you reach your goal ..."

- "What this really means for you is ..."

- "The benefit of this approach is that it makes things easier by ..."

- "Here's why this matters for what you're trying to achieve ..."

- "Here's how this solves the issue you mentioned earlier."

SECTION 7: Pressure-Free Transitions

These help you shift from one part of the conversation to the next without sounding abrupt or salesy. They protect the relationship while still keeping things moving.

- "Let me pause for a moment. Here's the next option if you'd like it ..."

- "If it makes sense, we can look at your options."

- "When you're ready, we can explore this further."

- "Here's something that might help. Want to hear it?"

- "If it's helpful, we can walk through the next step together."

SECTION 8: Objection Softeners and Resistance Reducers

These are designed to make people feel safe, not challenged. They lower tension and open the door to genuine conversation.

- "I hear what you're saying. Want to explore an alternative?"

- "We can go at your pace. What feels right to you?"

- "Would it help if we walked through that concern together?"

- "That makes sense. Want to look at another angle?"

- "It's completely up to you. Here's what might help."

- "No pressure. Just possibilities."

SECTION 9: Next-Step Invitations

These are the heart of the method. They make the next step clear while keeping the power of the decision in the hands of the other person.

"Would you like to explore this further?"

- "I'd be happy to show you what this could look like."

- "Want to take a look together?"

- "If you'd like help with this, I'd be happy to show you what that could look like."

- "If it makes sense, we can move forward from here."

- "What would you like to do next?"

SECTION 10: Leadership, Coaching, and Customer Service Invitations

These show support instead of authority. They create partnership, not pressure.

- "What direction feels right to you?"

- "Would you like my support on this?"

- "How can I best help right now?"

- "What would make progress feel easier for you?"

- "I can help with that if you'd like to take the next step."

- "Want to work through this together?"

SECTION 11: Everyday-Life Invitations

Invitational communication works everywhere.

These examples fit everyday situations and personal relationships.

- "This might be helpful. Want it?"

- "Here's an idea. Interested?"

- "If it helps, I can show you a simpler way."

- "Want me to take something off your plate?"

- "Would you like a suggestion?"

- "Want my opinion or just a listening ear?"

SECTION 12: From the Stage (for Speakers and Presenters)

These give your audience a clear invitation without ever sounding pushy or rushed. Perfect for keynotes, workshops, and training rooms.

- "If it feels right, you're invited to take the next step."

- "I'm not sure if this is right for you, but here's something that might help."

- "If you'd like to go deeper, here's how we can continue."

- "For those who want more support, here's the next step."

- "If this resonates, you're welcome to join us."

SECTION 13: Fill-in-the-Blank Templates

These simple structures make Invitational Selling™ easy to personalize for any situation or industry.

- "If you'd like support with _____, I can show you what the next step looks like."

- "Some clients choose _____, others choose _____. What feels right for you?"

- "Would it help if I walked you through _____?"

- "We can do this now or later. What works best for you?"

- "The benefit of _____ is _____. Would you like to explore that?"

- "If it makes sense, the next step would be _____. Want to take a look?"

You Do You

The phrases in this *Invitational Language Library*™ are here to guide you, not to box you in. Think of them as starting points and suggestions. Adapt them, personalize them, and expand them as you find your own rhythm and style. The more authentically these phrases sound coming from you, the more naturally others will respond.

Keep this library close, make it your own, and let every conversation become an opportunity to connect, to serve, and to offer a genuine invitation with clarity, confidence, and hear

ACKNOWLEDGMENTS

This book was written by one person, but shaped by many.

I am grateful to my family, thank you for being the grounding force behind everything I do.

Karen, thank you for your love and unwavering support, your wisdom, and your belief in me. Your encouragement, perspective, and steady presence have mattered more than you know.

To my son, Christopher, and my daughter-in-law, Kayla, thank you for your love and for the steady encouragement you have always shown.

Lauren, this book begins with you for a reason. Your courage, curiosity, and extraordinary spirit shaped the way I see connection, communication, and what truly matters. Invitational Selling™ exists because of what you taught me, through who you were. Your legacy lives on through these pages.

Jeffrey Hayzlett and the C-Suite Network, thank you for your leadership, partnership, and trust. Working together to grow the Corporate Speakers Council has been meaningful and energizing. I'm grateful for the opportunity to help advance conversations that matter at the highest levels.

To the members of the Corporate Speakers Council, thank you for the insight, professionalism, and generosity you bring to this community. Your willingness to engage, challenge ideas, and lead with intention continues to sharpen and strengthen this work.

To the Damon Brooks & Associates team and the Dani Pierre Agency, thank you for your belief in this message and for helping bring it to stages and audiences where it can make a real difference. Your advocacy and representation are truly appreciated.

Thanks to Katrina Nichols and to Anchor Point Press for their invaluable assistance with editing and publishing this work.

And finally, I would like to thank all my clients, audiences, and the leaders and organizations who have trusted me with your teams, your challenges, and your stories. Every conversation, keynote, workshop, and moment of insight has helped refine these ideas and bring Invitational Selling to life.

Stay Well and Stay Awesome,

Dennis

READER RESOURCES

Thank you for reading *Invitational Selling*™.

This book is designed to be practical, not theoretical. To support you in applying these ideas in real conversations, meetings, and sales situations, I've created a set of exclusive resources especially for readers.

These resources are meant to help you move from understanding the framework to using it with confidence and intention.

By scanning the QR code below, you'll have access to:

- A downloadable version of the **Invitational Selling™ Contextual Model**

- A visual reference for **Connect → Convey → Convert**

- Short conversational prompts designed to help you prepare for important conversations

- Additional tools and updates as this work continues to evolve

The resources are optional, complimentary, and designed to support your learning, not pressure you into next steps.

Scan the QR code below whenever you're ready.

https://www.denniscummins.com/invitational
-selling-reader-resources/

INTERESTED IN WORKING WITH DENNIS?

If the ideas in this book resonate with you and your organization, there are several ways to continue the conversation.

Dennis Cummins works with leaders, sales teams, and organizations through keynote presentations, workshops, and advisory engagements focused on communication, influence, and authentic connection in an AI-driven world.

For event planners: Dennis delivers high-impact keynote experiences designed to engage audiences, spark meaningful dialogue, and leave participants with practical takeaways they can use immediately.

His work is designed for organizations looking to:

- Strengthen leadership communication

- Improve sales conversations without pressure

- Align teams around clarity, trust, and purpose

- Build messages that connect with real people, not just algorithms

To learn more about Dennis's speaking, consulting, or training programs, visit:

www.DennisCummins.com

You may access additional resources and the most current offerings by scanning the QR code below.

ABOUT THE AUTHOR

Dennis Cummins is a **sought-after Thought Leader**, keynote speaker, consultant, and communication strategist who helps sales professionals, business owners, and organizations drive results through genuine human connection in an increasingly automated marketplace.

As the creator of the Invitational Selling™ framework, Dennis teaches a people-first approach to sales communication that replaces pressure-based persuasion with clarity, trust, and authentic invitation. His work helps individuals and teams cut through sameness, build credibility faster, and create conversations that lead naturally to buy-in and action.

Dennis brings decades of real-world experience working with sales teams, executives, and entrepreneurs across industries. He is the founder of Pro Speaker Academy and serves as Co-Chairman of the Corporate Speakers Council within the C-Suite Network, where he supports leaders and sales professionals in strengthening influence, communication, and commercial impact.

The ideas in this book are shaped by his professional experience and everyday life. Dennis's daughter, Lauren, whose story opens this book, profoundly influenced how he understands connection, resilience, and what it means to truly see another person. Her legacy lives at the heart of Invitational Selling™.

Today, Dennis continues to speak, teach, and consult with organizations committed to improving sales performance, building trust at scale, and communicating in ways that respect autonomy while consistently driving results.

www.ingramcontent.com/pod-product-compliance
Lightning Source LLC
Chambersburg PA
CBHW051343280526
45784CB00007B/2790